Achievement for All in International Classrooms

Achievement for All in International Classrooms

Improving Outcomes for Children and Young People with Special Educational Needs and Disabilities

SONIA BLANDFORD

Bloomsbury Academic
An imprint of Bloomsbury Publishing Plc

B L O O M S B U R Y
LONDON · OXFORD · NEW YORK · NEW DELHI · SYDNEY

Bloomsbury Academic

An imprint of Bloomsbury Publishing Plc

50 Bedford Square
London
WC1B 3DP
UK

1385 Broadway
New York
NY 10018
USA

www.bloomsbury.com

BLOOMSBURY and the Diana logo are trademarks of Bloomsbury Publishing Plc

First published 2017

British Library Cataloguing-in-Publication Data
A catalogue record for this book is available from the British Library.

ISBN: HB: 978-1-4742-5432-8
PB: 978-1-4742-5433-5
ePDF: 978-1-4742-5435-9
ePub: 978-1-4742-5434-2

Library of Congress Cataloging-in-Publication Data
A catalog record for this book is available from the Library of Congress.

Cover image: © Blend Images - KidStock / Getty Images

Typeset by Deanta Global Publishing Services, Chennai, India
Printed and bound in Great Britain

To Charlie, Bethany and Mia,
for your support of Achievement for All

CONTENTS

LIST OF FIGURES

FOREWORD

This book and its predecessor, *Achievement for All: Raising Aspirations, Access and Achievement* (Bloomsbury, 2013), are about a revolution in education and in ways of thinking about children with Special Education Needs and Disability (SEND). Achievement for All was born out of an intense frustration that the education system still accepted that children with SEND would not achieve their full potential, and policy and practice did not challenge this. Achievement for All is a movement in education, which aims to transform our aspirations and ways of working. It aims to bring together the best of what educators know and do into one overall programme to achieve better outcomes for the most vulnerable children. It joins this with our best understanding of how better parental engagement in their children's education can improve attainment and outcomes. Achievement for All puts teaching and teachers back in the centre of education practice. Above all, the Achievement for All programme is about transforming the aspirations of schools, parents and young people to believe that they can become the best that they can be.

This philosophy has been embodied in a programme and organization, which has developed that approach and demonstrated its effectiveness across the English education system since 2009. Part of that journey has also been learning from and demonstrating how the same approach could be adapted and progressed in different countries. This had been a remarkable international collaboration with educators in many different countries and circumstances. The golden thread that runs through this initiative is the values and aspirations of the Achievement for All programme and the passion and vision of Sonia Blandford and the expert group of educators and committed professionals she has gathered together to enable this vision.

This book is the collected wisdom of that process and learning. Sonia Blandford brings together practical examples of implementation in a number of different settings with wide-ranging thinking about what an inclusive and progressive education system can and must do to ensure that any country's future generation can thrive. The international debate about education is dominated by what place countries occupy in the Organisation for Economic Co-operation and Development Programme for International Student Assessment (OECD PISA) tables. The OECD's **PISA rankings** compare the test results of fifteen-year-olds in different countries on the basis of regional education systems in mathematics and reading. Yet we know that the countries that do best are those with the most inclusive systems of education which embody the highest aspirations for all their children and value the role that parents and professionals play in working together to achieve better outcomes. This book embodies the key lessons for any education system which wants to move towards the goal of *Achievement for All* for our children.

Brian Lamb OBE, Chair of Achievement for All and Visiting Professor of SEND, Derby University, UK

ACKNOWLEDGEMENTS

Writing a book of this magnitude covering no less than seven nations has been a team endeavour. I am grateful to Dr Catherine Knowles for her considerable ability in researching and collaborating on the presentation of the final text, and to Dr Dean West and Maureen Hunt for their comments and contributions. I am also grateful to my Achievement for All colleagues who have led the way in innovation, commitment and collective responsibility for the continued development of the Achievement for All programme.

Across the globe, I have been supported by many leaders, policy makers, teachers, parents and carers, children and young people. My thanks to you all for many contributions to engaging in the delivery and research that make up the rich and varied accounts reported in this book.

Beginning in England and Wales, the Achievement for All programme would not have been possible without the recommendation of the 2009 Lamb Inquiry, led by our chair, Brian Lamb, whose contribution to positive developments in special educational needs provision is recognized widely across the globe. A shared vision and common-sense approach to even the most difficult challenges, needs and disadvantages has led us both to committing much time and dedication to Achievement for All. My thanks to Brian for his guidance and wise counsel in establishing the charity from which these projects have originated.

Egle Pranckuniene and Marina Vildziuniene from the Centre for School Improvement, Vilnius, Lithuania, supported by Dr Coleen Jackson and the Achievement for All 3As project, have transformed leadership across Lithuania. This was summarized by Egle: 'Faster than history, slower than a lifetime'. Thank you for the opportunity to develop the 3As vision that underpins our joint work.

Leadership is also a theme central to the work of 'Mission Possible' in Latvia, founded and led by Zane Olina, a magical mother of four with a huge heart. Thank you for your generosity and wisdom in creating our shared approach to leading learning.

Astrid Songen and Vibeke Strom of the Oslo Kommune provided the opportunity to deliver the Achievement for All in Oslo, Norway, led by our colleague achievement coach, Heather Daulphin. This was where the impact on parental engagement and teaching and learning has been profound. Thank you for your commitment to all children and the development of your schools.

A small-scale project in New York was the result of GEMS Education Foundation's funded activity led by Chris Kirk and the parent group including the *Beyond the Bake Sale* author Anne Henderson. This led to Achievement for All being commissioned to participate in a truly memorable community conference hosted by Mayor Bill de Blasio, in recognition of our global standing in parental engagement, co-delivered with Melanie Warnes, national leader of education, Principal, British School, Belgium. Thank you for the opportunity to share our knowledge and understanding of this important issue. Thanks also for the detailed research that features in Chapter 10.

The development of the Achievement for All programme in Wales was made possible by a partnership with the Wales Centre for Equity in Education, Trinity St David, University of Wales led by Professor David Egan. The significance of this activity has been recognized by the Welsh Assembly and Hugh Lewis, minister for education and skills. Such is the commitment of my Welsh colleagues that the programme continues to extend its reach and grow in impact. Thank you for your insight, wisdom and commitment to closing the poverty gap in Wales (and for teaching and guiding us on the 'Welshness of Wales').

Kevin Skeoch and his senior leadership team at Dwight International School in Seoul, South Korea, invited me to develop inclusive middle leadership in this inspiring setting, which led to a small-scale research project and a number of blogs. Thank you for your participation and leadership.

Beyond the national and international innovations and sharing, I have to thank the team at Bloomsbury for inviting me to write this collection of delivery and research projects. Thank you for your support throughout the process and for your creativity in developing the final publication.

My final thanks is to my family, Charlie, Bethany and Mia whose endless patience and care has provided me with the stability needed to create, write and travel. All authors' profits are to be donated to Achievement for All, registered charity 1142154.

Introduction

This book is written for education students, practitioners and policy makers committed to improving outcomes for all children and young people. The intention being to provide an introduction to the Achievement for All framework and the 3As principles: Aspiration, Access and Achievement.

Having the opportunity to develop, introduce, implement and evaluate the Achievement for All framework through programme delivery in England, Wales, Norway and America and the 3As principles in Lithuania, Latvia and South Korea has been a unique experience for the author. The number of leaders, teachers, parents and carers, children and young people engaged in the projects described in this book exceeds two million. This includes the largest study of its kind in Europe (Achievement for All pilot, 2009–11) and smaller-scale research in American schools.

The research and evaluation methodologies differ in each context and investigation, the common factors being the engagement with leaders, teachers, parents and carers, children and young people in gathering their views and, where possible determining progress. This book therefore provides an insight into research possibilities available to education practitioners on a daily basis. The depth of each investigation has also differed; extensive quantitative and qualitative evaluations have informed the chapters focusing on England, Wales, Lithuania, Norway and America. A more ethnographic, descriptive approach is taken in the context of leadership development in Latvia and South Korea.

The Achievement for All framework contains four elements: leadership, teaching and learning, parent and carer engagement, and wider opportunities. Each of these four elements is featured where the programme has been delivered in full (England, Wales and Norway). Other country settings have provided the opportunity to develop individual elements: parent and carer engagement in America and leadership in Lithuania. Further examination of the 3As principles – Aspiration, Access and Achievement – has also been made possible through leadership development in Latvia and South Korea. The framework is used to structure the main sections of the book. As a consequence of the bespoke nature of the partnerships in each country, the sections are not of equal length, but are designed to provide an insight into the potential of the Achievement for All framework and 3As principles within national contexts.

The engagement of each country with the Achievement for All framework, programme and/or 3As principles has been on self-selecting. The author, and the Achievement for All 3As charity and research colleagues were selected via competitive tender (England and Wales) or invited by Ministries of Education or their representatives (America, Latvia, South Korea, Lithuania and Norway) to develop, introduce or deliver projects in each country setting. The roles of the author, Achievement for All coaches and school leaders have been collaborative, generating a network committed to improving outcomes of the most vulnerable children and young people, those that have needs and face challenge and disadvantage on a daily basis.

The level of participation by leaders, teachers, parents and carers, children and young people within education settings has proven to be significant with 100 per cent responses to surveys, interviews and focus group requests. Data has been gathered by a central team, independently validated and evaluated by universities (England, America and Lithuania), PwC strategy team based in Northern Ireland (England and Wales), ministerial teams (Latvia, Norway, Lithuania) and school leadership teams (South Korea).

Motivated by the need for change in the approaches taken to improve the outcomes of all children and young people, the author has been privileged to partner with committed, visionary leaders prepared to take risks on behalf of those identified with special needs or disability, the challenged and disadvantaged. United Nations data (2010) states that while children form only 20 per cent of the world's population, they are also 100 per cent of the world's future. Failure to invest in change for the one in five children who is vulnerable remains an issue for many leaders in schools and those in local and national government.

This book will provide an insight into what can happen when leaders embrace change, however difficult, in varying contexts. All children and young people deserve a future, we need to find their greatness, dig it out and enable them to share it with the world.

PART ONE

An International Issue: Bringing Special Educational Needs and Disability (SEND) Back into the Classroom

CHAPTER ONE

The Achievement for All Framework

I think Achievement for All has enabled us to focus on narrowing the gap for the pupils rather than just supporting pupils. I think what we have been guilty of perhaps is identifying SEND and supporting them in school but not challenging their potential and I think Achievement for All has actually taken our good practice and challenged it and made us take that step a bit further.

(LEAD TEACHER, ENGLAND, IN A SCHOOL USING THE ACHIEVEMENT FOR ALL FRAMEWORK)

The Achievement for All programme in practice

Achievement for All is an international education charity based in England, founded and led by Professor Sonia Blandford since 2011, the same year in which it won a competitive tender to lead the national roll-out of the Achievement for All programme. The programme provides schools with an intensive two-year leadership development and staff training programme, led by expert coaches and designed to transform the education outcomes and life chances of children and young people vulnerable to underachievement. Based on a similar model to that of the Achievement for All pilot (2009–11), also led by Professor Sonia Blandford, in which 454 schools across England participated, the current programme is continuing to demonstrate a huge impact on the academic and wider outcomes of children and young people vulnerable to underachievement. The programme is founded on the vision of a world in which all children and young people can achieve regardless of their background, challenge or need, and this is realized by transforming lives through improved educational opportunities and outcomes.

In evaluating the Achievement for All pilot in England (2009–11), the University of Manchester completed one of the largest studies of a programme for children identified with SEND in Europe. To assist with the next stage of the development and roll-out of the programme, they recommended the following:

- There should be a strong focus on school-led improvement in order to transform the outcomes for children with SEND. The most successful schools in the pilot had strong leadership from the head teacher or senior leadership team, rather than relying purely on the SEN coordinator (SENCo).

- Teachers should carry out regular target reviews with parents to monitor progress of children and assess where extra help may be required.

- Regular, scheduled conversations on educational outcomes between parents and teachers should take place, with teachers given extra training in managing these relationships.

- Schools should build on existing good practice and share ideas between schools, as this is when the Achievement for All programme is most successful.

This chapter provides an introduction to the Achievement for All framework and 3As principles: Aspiration, Access and Achievement that have been developed across seven nations, exploring the Achievement for All school programmes and considering its merits as an effective model for inclusion leading to school improvement.

Achievement for All framework: Four elements

The Achievement for All programme, delivered collaboratively with school leaders, teachers, SENCos, parents, carers, children and young people and other professionals in primary, secondary, special schools and pupil referral units, provides a bespoke framework for school improvement. Building on current school practices, the framework is implemented and developed through the following four interdependent key elements:

1 **Leadership of school, classroom and teams; teaching and learning.**

   A focus on consolidating, supporting and developing a culture of distributed, inclusive and effective leadership throughout the school community.

2   Teaching and Learning: assessment and data tracking, planning and delivery

A focus on closing the gap, by developing more effective teaching for all children in their classroom and more effective and holistic provision mapping.

3   Parent and carer engagement: structured conversations; listening to parents.

A focus on raising aspiration and achievement and removing barriers to learning by developing positive and constructive partnerships between parents and carers and schools.

4   Wider outcomes and opportunities: improving behaviour, attendance and participation in school life.

A focus on securing children's engagement across the curriculum and wider provision, developing behaviours for learning, attendance and well-being and supporting pupils' personal resilience.

Schools elect to join the programme, funded in part by national and local government grants, including the Pupil Premium, and directly by the school. After registration, an Achievement for All coach is allocated and a school 'champion' appointed internally. The approach is strongly collaborative and, following an initial gap analysis, areas across the school, where change would be beneficial to pupil outcomes, are identified. Target groups are selected from the lowest achieving 20 per cent including those with SEND, those looked after by the state, and children and young people from socio-economic disadvantage.

The Achievement for All programme in practice

The Achievement for All programme is based on in-depth interaction, dialogue, and co-construction between the staff and leadership of the participant school (including a named school champion drawn from the senior leadership team of the school), and an expert network of Achievement for All coaches.

An achievement coach is appointed by Achievement for All, from among a team of highly experienced, outstanding, and in many cases nationally recognized, school leaders and practitioners. In England, this includes a number of Local Leaders of Education (LLE) and National Leaders of Education (NLE). The Achievement for All coaches are supported by regional leads (all of whom are highly innovative and effective teachers, leaders, and practitioners) and many of whom led the pilot in their local authorities.

The partnership between schools, the school champion and the Achievement for All coaches is designed to

- establish an initial needs analysis and identification of the pupil target group in the school.
- support the school in creating and implementing a programme plan, bolstered and informed by a set of bi-weekly, half-day visits over two years.
- facilitate three whole-school training days over two years.
- integrate the school into an overlapping set of communities of practice with thousands of other schools.

This partnership is underpinned by a simple 'virtuous circle' of activity in schools, which include:

- Achievement for All coaches contribute to developing the skills of school staff.
- Achievement for All coaches help school staff to hold effective structured conversations with parents and carers.
- School staff develop their teaching and learning strategies, informed by Achievement for All coaches, which are designed to increase opportunities for the target young people.
- School colleagues evaluate outcomes.
- Outcomes are expanded to all pupils.
- Outcomes are fed into the development of school staff.

Schools can expect evidence from the programme in the following ways:

Quantitative

- A closing of the achievement gap for pupils with SEND and other pupils who are vulnerable to underachievement.
- Pupils in target groups making more progress than these groups nationally.
- Accelerated progress across reading, writing and maths for pupils in target groups.
- Fewer exclusions have been evidenced in the majority of schools, providing significant savings in staff time and obvious benefits in education outcomes for pupils.
- Better attendance for all participating pupils, impacting on learning, behaviour and progress.

Qualitative

- Schools enabled to address the specific needs of their staff, parents and carers and pupils. The bespoke nature of the programme is perhaps its most unique feature.
- Development of a better culture of aspiration and engagement, leading to more focused lessons.
- Better teaching and learning across the school.
- Better behaviour for learning across the school.
- Planning for children with SEND is more pupil- and parent-centred.
- An increase in pupil confidence and aspiration.
- Increased parent and carer engagement.
- School leaders committed to maximizing the potential of the programme in terms of its capacity to impact at an individual level, a whole-school level and at a partnership level with other schools.
- Structured conversations feeding into more effective planning, which enables schools to deliver more personalized teaching and learning. In addition, parents and staff work more effectively together to address the individual needs of each child.
- A strategic focus on ensuring high-quality teaching and learning. More staff training and better dissemination of good practice.
- More effective monitoring and tracking of pupils with SEND and others vulnerable to underachievement.
- A strategic focus on planning and implementing additional activities (and identification of gaps in provision) for SEND pupils and others vulnerable to underachievement.

(Source: Reported by the PwC Achievement for All monitoring and evaluation team between September 2011 and December 2012)

3As principles – Increasing aspiration and access leading to higher achievement

The four interdependent elements are underpinned by the 3As principles to increase the aspirations, access and achievement of children and young people with SEND and others that are vulnerable to underachievement.

- *Aspiration* encompasses the expectations, beliefs, understanding and capacity of learners to engage fully and positively in the learning process. It is the mindset that underpins all educational endeavours, whereby practitioners, parents/carers and learners have a shared understanding of that which can be achieved through the setting of goals (short-, medium- and long-term), culminating in the raising of aspirations.

- *Access* has a twofold meaning. The first is the removal of barriers preventing access to learning; these can be broad or specific, for example, low expectations, physiological, social, environmental, educational and more. The second meaning is the provision of education, compulsory, further and higher, and for those who might not have previously perceived education as having any significance or value in their lives.

- *Achievement* is a term that has been devalued by the political drive to 'count' examination results as an indicator of educational success or attainment. While it is essential that the workforce is literate and numerate, knowing what achievement is, having the self-efficacy to achieve and recognizing when this happens is fundamental to learning. Achievement lies within and extends beyond exams: social, artistic, musical, sporting and leadership endeavours all count towards the achievement for all. It is the breadth of success that facilitates the application of learning.

Summary

For many schools the Achievement for All programme has offered a chance to reflect on how they approach the issues that confront these pupils, prompting them to find new and innovative ways of solving them. Behaviour is an essential factor in determining how pupils make progress in their learning and access the wider opportunities of school life. However, the 'intricate and profound' link between behavioural standards and SEND (Steer, 2009) means these pupils may find it harder to achieve appropriate behaviour for learning. Achievement for All has worked with schools to improve the behaviour of pupils identified with SEND and others vulnerable to underachievement. By improving how they communicate with parents and carers, Achievement for All has also allowed schools in multiple settings to identify previously unknown barriers to learning, leading to greater achievement once they have been broken down. Greater engagement has empowered parents and carers to take an active role in their children's learning, meaning progress becomes more sustainable and schools, parents and pupils hold greater aspirations about what can be achieved. Evidence from the programme and adoption of the 3As principles illustrates how the simplest of acts, whether these are communication or pedagogy, can increase participation in learning and enhance the life chances of all pupils.

The following chapter focuses on the rationale and approach taken by the Achievement for All charity in extending its work across England and Wales. Focusing on inclusion, the chapter considers the importance of leadership in implementing change that will impact on the life chances of children and young people identified with special needs and those with disabilities. The implications of committing to a framework and the 3As principles can be positive, as the case studies presented throughout this book will attest.

CHAPTER TWO

Why the Approach to SEND in Schools across the World Needs to Change

The world is both big and small depending on where you have been and where you are going; we all have a responsibility to encourage learning and to find the greatness that exists in everyone.

(BLANDFORD, 2015)

Government policy across nation states, although aimed at helping educators and other stakeholders to identify and assess SEND, often lacks the clarity or depth needed for practice; this leads to confusion as to how it should be developed in schools (Gibson and Blandford, 2005). This is further impacted by inconsistencies in terminology across countries around the definition of SEND and its assessment, leaving it much open to interpretation at the local level. In part, interpretations of SEND explain the relatively large differences in the proportion of pupils identified with SEND across countries, as determined by legislation and provision.

As a result, many question the inconsistency in views and attitudes towards the meaning of inclusion, which may explain, in part, the nurturing of what some researchers and practitioners consider to be non-inclusive practices (O'Gorman and Drudy, 2010; Pujol, 2010). Recognizing effective links between policy and practice for the implementation of inclusion (Blandford, 2006) has strong implications for practice. This chapter will consider the origins and meaning of inclusive education, a focus relevant to both policy and practice.

Inclusive education

The movement towards inclusive education has been a global phenomenon, as demonstrated in the fundamental philosophy and key practice of the United Nations International Children's Emergency Fund (UNICEF) and the United Nations Education, Science and Cultural Organization (UNESCO, 1994, 2005). UK government policy has promoted inclusive education since the Warnock Report (HMSO, 1978). Ruijs et al. (2010: 352), reflecting the Salamanca Agreement (UNESCO, 1994), broadly define inclusive education as the education of children with special educational needs (SEN) in a 'regular' school instead of a special school. Despite the increasing importance of inclusive education on the global agenda, Pujol (2010) is critical of the prominence of 'segregated' education in some countries. He contrasts the significant place of special schools and classes in the Netherlands with the reduced number of pupils in special education in Norway in recent years.

The Lamb Inquiry (DCSF, 2009) and the national delivery of the Achievement for All programme (DfE, 2011) in England marked a turning point for SEND policy and practice, placing it more firmly within the domain of school leadership and bringing greater focus to inclusive education. Founded on the principle of removing barriers to learning and participation (Booth and Ainscow, 2002), inclusive education is most appropriately delineated within a framework for practice; its indistinct boundaries (Ainscow et al., 2004) tend to preclude a precise definition. This may, in part, explain the vagueness of the way it has been promoted and articulated in government policy. In practice, inclusive education encompasses such areas as school cultures, policies and practices, child and parental voice and achieving potential (DfES, 2001). The Centre for Studies on Inclusive Education (CSIE) (2011) outlines what this involves in an educational setting:

- valuing all students and staff equally

- increasing the participation of students in, and reducing their exclusion from, the cultures, curricula and communities of local schools

- restructuring the cultures, policies and practices in schools so that they respond to the diversity of students in the locality

- reducing barriers to learning and participation for all students, not only those with impairments or those who are categorized as 'having special educational needs'

- learning from attempts to overcome barriers to the access and participation of particular students to make changes for the benefit of students more widely

- viewing the difference between students as resources to support learning, rather than as problems to be overcome

- acknowledging the right of students to an education in their locality

- improving schools for staff as well as for students

- emphasizing the role of schools in building community and developing values, as well as in increasing achievement

- fostering mutually sustaining relationships between schools and communities

- recognizing that inclusion in education is one aspect of inclusion in society.

Inclusive education initiatives, however, have tended to focus on aspects of inclusion (Ainscow et al., 2004) rather than taking a whole-school approach or addressing change at systems level. Effective inclusive education in schools may call for change in both practices and attitudes.

Whole-school commitment to inclusion has been fundamental to the development of Achievement for All in England and consequently in its place in the six other nations described in this book. Throughout this work, vision, commitment, collaboration and the communication of an inclusive message underpinned by an inclusive ethos have provided unprecedented change to the lives of children and young people identified with special needs and those with disabilities.

Leading inclusion

Research literature emphasizes the central role of school leaders in shaping inclusive education (Kugelmass, 2003; Kugelmass and Ainscow, 2004). This points towards leadership for inclusion, which is central to the Achievement for All initiative. Gold et al. (2003: 18) place this within the context of transformational models of leadership (Bass, 1999), characterized by 'inclusivity' and 'teacher participation'. Evidence from a pilot study across thirteen schools in Cyprus exploring inclusion in the context of leadership highlighted the central role of the leader in the development of inclusive education and the place of distributed leadership in developing inclusion (Angelides, 2010).

Arrowsmith (2007: 22) loosely defines distributed leadership as 'an emerging form of power distribution in schools which extends authority and influence to groups or individuals in a way which is at least partly contrary to hierarchical arrangements'. This provides an appropriate framework in which to consider the distribution of leadership in the Achievement for All framework, where practices vary according to leadership style and context. In addition, the multiple 'usages' of distributed leadership (Mayrowetz, 2008) and their differing views (Spillane 2006; Gronn, 2000) tend to preclude the delineation of distributed leadership within a narrow framework. Nonetheless, Arrowsmith (2007: 24), in his small-scale case study research exploring head teacher roles in the development of distributed leadership in six secondary schools in England, highlighted a number of common head teacher 'actions' conducive to its development. These were cited as 'effective communication across the school, structures, advocacy to individuals, encouraging words, staff appointments, defined outcomes and the development of trust'.

Spillane (2006) suggests that distributed leadership becomes operational through the interactions of people in their context. What is critical, he further suggests, is not that leadership is distributed, but *how* it is distributed. This is largely manifested through leadership style, which in inclusive schools is collaborative in approach (Kugelmass, 2003; Kugelmass and Ainscow, 2004). Although this suggests a transformational model of leadership, Campbell et al. (2003: 205), citing Silins (1994), suggest that effective school leaders adopt aspects of both transformational and transactional leadership practice in school improvement. What characterizes the leadership approach in implementing and developing Achievement for All in schools is not the strong commitment of leaders to vision but the proactive sharing of the development of that vision with staff, parents and children in developing commitment across the school. In the majority of schools this has been manifested through transformational models of leadership of which vision is a central component (Bass, 1999).

Achievement for All with its particular focus on effective inclusive leadership, centred on moral purpose (Fullan, 2007), improves outcomes for children and sustainability and rightly sets it within the wider field of educational leadership encompassing leading change, building capacity and leading systems (Fullan, 2004). In providing a framework in which leaders, teaching and other school staff consider how to work more effectively with the child as the focus, Achievement for All offers opportunity for leading reforms from within (Hopkins, 2007; Carter et al., 2006). Running parallel to the drive for change across schools is the increased interest in systems leadership (Fullan, 2004). This brings leadership into the broader context of building structures, processes and cultures, which act on the system as a whole (O'Leary and Craig, 2007).

Harris and Muijs (2005: 37), however, suggest that the 'success' of change is related to the extent to which an educational organization builds 'capacity for change and development'. Fullan (2005: 69) is critical of accepting 'capacity building' on a theoretical level alone, suggesting that professional development needs to be coupled with the daily habit of 'working together' 'and having mechanisms for getting better at it on purpose'. This is particularly relevant in the context of SEND, where literature highlights the need for both training and experience of inclusive education for the development of positive attitudes (Pujol, 2010).

Achievement for All encourages and promotes an inclusive approach to education. Inclusion acknowledges the impact of the social environment upon children's abilities to learn and develop. It seeks to facilitate diversity and to ensure that pupils' needs are viewed equitably and met fairly (Ainscow, 1999). Leadership in Achievement for All schools is founded on a framework developed by the NCSL (2009) for the successful leadership and management of SEND. Based on international research in inclusive education (Kugelmass 2003; Beany 2006) and other NCSL research, four key elements were identified as being central to inclusive leadership – shared vision, commitment, collaboration and communication (NCSL, 2009: 6). A central theme of the initiative is that of effective leadership practice for SEND provision. Creating an inclusive school involves the coming together of policy and practice, in that policy is informed by practice through review and practitioner engagement. As practitioners we should ask the question, 'If we were to shine a light on every pupil, how many would not be able to make progress?' The answer is, of course, none. All pupils have the potential to make progress in school.

The underlying 3As principles of Aspiration, Access and Achievement enable leaders and teachers, parents and carers to improve outcomes for all children and young people. Before moving to a detailed analysis of the Achievement for All programme and 3As principles in England and Wales, the following case study describes how the 3As were applied to the context of educational development in Latvia.

Latvia: Developing education

During 2012–14, the author was invited to deliver a series of lectures to Mission Possible students, higher education teacher educators and policy leaders from the Latvian ministry of education. The presentations focused on the 3A principles – Aspiration, Access and Achievement.

Maximizing impact by developing Achievement, Access and Aspirations: A model for practice

School leaders and teachers can have a profound impact on all children and young people by developing their Achievement, Access and Aspirations. An effective teacher increases Access and raises Aspirations as a means to improving Achievement. An inspirational teacher improves Achievement in a way that changes learners' Aspirations, and in doing so improves their life chances by securing Access to continued Achievement and self-fulfilment. Aspiration, Access and Achievement are each broad terms for multiple mediating factors on an individual's life chances.

It is important for education that there is an educational system where Aspiration, Access and Achievement apply to all learners. All teachers, leaders and support professionals need to collaborate to provide a system where the importance of education is understood and valued by all pupils and their parents.

The Achievement for All vision for education is a system that raises the Aspirations of all pupils, supported by parents, teachers, leaders and professionals, providing Access to schools that inspire, drive and inform learning for all pupils, the outcome being Achievement for all. Underpinning the vision of achievement for all are the 3As needed to drive practice in schools:

Aspiration

Aspiration relates to having high expectations about what learners can achieve. It reflects a 'can do' mentality displayed when a pupil decides to meet challenges and gain access to learning, thus believing that they can succeed. Pupils identified with SEND and others vulnerable to underachievement may reduce their aspirations and consequently become demotivated. Pupils with low aspirations do not always hold their future in high regard and may not have a vision for further education or extracurricular activities. Achievement for All works with schools to raise aspirations, focusing in particular on attitudes, parental aspiration, motivation and school and teacher aspiration.

A pupil's mindset can greatly affect their desire to access school, achieve and improve their future. Pupils can be disengaged or negative for a number of reasons, ranging from established family views about education to their previous experiences in school. Parental engagement has a very distinct and wide-reaching effect on pupil aspirations. Parents with low aspirations often unintentionally pass their beliefs and feelings on to their children. Furthermore, parents who do not understand the education system may struggle to communicate aspirations to their children. Without good modelling of an aspirational outlook, it can be difficult for children to have their own aspirations. It is important that pupils with SEND and others vulnerable to underachievement feel motivated, not only to overcome potential barriers but so that they continue to have aspirations about what they are able to achieve. In order for pupils to become aspirational in the school environment or to continue to raise their aspirations, it is crucial for staff to be aspirational for them. Without a whole-school culture which models aspirational values and holds a strong belief in the pupils' abilities to access and achieve, it is difficult for them to do so.

The Achievement for All programme has supported leaders and teachers and other staff in raising aspirations across the school. By increasing pupil confidence through various initiatives, the staff have worked to change mindsets and attitudes. Parents' aspirations have been raised by sharing their children's achievements and having structured conversations with schools, allowing them to become fully involved in supporting their children through education. The stigma often associated with SEND can be reduced by focusing on whole-school aspirations, so that teachers and leaders become part of and encourage a culture in which all can achieve and progress by setting aspirational targets and having high expectations. By raising pupil, parent and teacher aspirations, schools can also help learners to access opportunities and begin to encourage them to focus on specific areas, such as classroom behaviour, attendance and extracurricular activities, in order to help pupils gain access to education and feel part of an inclusive culture.

Access

The innovative approach, promoted and supported by the Achievement for All framework, enables schools to help break down barriers which often prevent children and young people with SEND and others vulnerable to underachievement, from accessing all the opportunities schools has to offer. Many schools have found that the Achievement for All programme has allowed them to improve the access these pupils have to the curriculum, leading to increased enjoyment of learning, greater aspirations and higher levels of achievement. Just as importantly, it has enabled pupils to access extracurricular activities through which they develop positive relationships and enjoy increased participation in school life.

Achievement

There is a tendency to focus achievement on attainment, experience of success, progress and recognition. This is relevant to practice and would include: goals set as a foundation for raising achievement that are within reach and achievable while not lowering expectations. **Strategies** are developed that can generate **outcomes** which provide a catalyst for an **impact** which may appear several years later.

However, achievement can be applied to contexts that are beyond attainment. A sense of well-being, resilience, self-efficacy and self-respect are all fundamental to achievement. For all children and young people, it is the feeling of success that is important; leaders and teachers, parents and carers should begin from the assumption of achievement for all.

The following diagram illustrates the interrelatedness of each of the 3As.

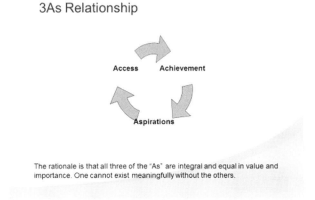

3As Relationship

Access   Achievement

Aspirations

The rationale is that all three of the "As" are integral and equal in value and importance. One cannot exist meaningfully without the others.

FIGURE 2.1 *3As principles – Aspiration, Access, Achievement*

It is important to recognize the cyclical relationship of each element in Figure 2.1. All the three 'As' are integral and equal in value; one cannot exist meaningfully without the others. An effective teacher increases Access and raises Aspirations as a means to improving Achievement. An inspirational teacher improves Achievement in a way that changes a pupil's Aspirations, and in doing so improves their life chances by securing Access to continued Achievement and self-fulfilment.

Summary

Inclusion is a global phenomenon, one that applies to all countries regardless of culture. Leaders have the power to include; teachers, parents and carers have the capacity to educate children and young people to be inclusive.

Policy changes in England and Wales made provision for Achievement for All in both nations, as a pilot and through the first phase of a national roll-out. The following chapters provide a policy and research summary describing the context and impact of the introduction of the Achievement for All programme in England and Wales. The flexibility of the framework is demonstrable by the bespoke nature of the delivery, led by experienced school leaders through model of coaching support.

PART TWO

Beginning with Achievement for All in England and Wales

CHAPTER THREE

England and Wales: Differing Contexts

In both England and Wales today, there are too many children and young people (CYP) who are not fulfilling their potential, and are also unhappy at school. CYP with Special Educational Needs and Disability (SEND), Looked After Children (LAC), pupils eligible for Free School Meals (FSM) and others vulnerable to underachievement are most likely to:

- experience various levels of commitment and support from school leaders, teachers and wider professionals.
- experience bullying at school.
- have poor school attendance.
- fail to gain academic qualifications and gain access to further or higher education.

(Blandford and Knowles, 2013)

The achievement gap between the 1.3 million (18 per cent) pupils identified with SEN in England compared with those without SEN is as wide as 41 per cent at each Key Stage (KS) (DfE, 2015) and although the gap has closed slightly over recent years, it remains stubbornly high. This compares with Wales, where 105,000 children and young people are on the SEN register; this amounts to almost one in five learners. Although the achievement gaps for children and young people with SEN in Wales are smaller than in England (2014: 29 per cent at KS2 and 36 per cent at KS4), their peers without SEN have a lower achievement level than this group in England. In addition, unlike England, where the achievement gaps at each Key Stage have closed slightly in the last few years, the achievement gap at KS4 in Wales has changed little since 2010 (National Assembly for Wales, 2015).

The Lamb Inquiry (2009) for the government in England exposed failures in the SEN system, parents' frustrations and too great a focus on processes rather than outcomes. During his inquiry into parental confidence, Brian Lamb often discussed with parents the aspirations they had for their children. They told him two things:

- they wanted better outcomes for their children
- they wanted their children to be valued for the contribution they could make.

Effective engagement of parents leads to a profound impact on children's progress and to a mutual trust between parents and school. When this is absent, outcomes decline and confidence in the school and the SEND system drains away. The educational achievement for children with SEND is too low and the gap with their peers is too wide. Failure to give children with SEND the same chance to reach their potential as other children represents a huge loss of talent and society ends up footing the bill. This tragic failure to realize children's potential and parents' aspirations has a long history. A system was needed that valued children with SEND, a system that:

- encourages aspiration and provides children with the support to achieve better outcomes, helping them strive to be the best they can be
- welcomes parents as valued partners in improving outcomes for their children
- values children with SEND, ensuring that they are welcome and happy members of their school community.

Out of this desire to ensure that children with SEND are not failed in the future, Achievement for All was born. This chapter will explore the differing contexts and the history of SEND in England and Wales and consider the extent to which the climate was ripe for Achievement for All.

SEND: The English context

The Lamb Inquiry (2009) marked a turning point for SEND, placing it more firmly within the domain of school leadership and bringing greater focus to inclusive education. In 2008, Lamb was commissioned to make recommendations on how provision could be improved for SEND learners. His core recommendations included changing the way SEND is identified, making schools more accountable for the progress of low achieving learners and supporting schools in setting high aspirations for all, focusing on attainment, engaging parents and developing wider outcomes. The recommendations are embodied in the Achievement for All programme.

During the Achievement for All pilot (2009–11) the programme was further endorsed in the SEN Green Paper – *Support and Aspiration: A new approach to special educational needs and disability* (DfE, 2011), which acknowledged it as an effective means of enabling children with SEND to achieve 'better educational outcomes and accelerated progress'. The document outlined proposals for a cultural change including personalized budgets for parents and carers, an Education, Health and Care Plan (replacing Statements) and a single assessment process, replacing School Action and School Action Plus.

The report that summarized the responses to the Green Paper, *Support and Aspiration: A new approach to special educational needs and disability – Progress and next steps* (DfE, 2012) recommended the national roll-out of the programme 'to ensure schools have access to what works well'. The document also emphasized the centrality of identifying children's needs early, giving head teachers the opportunity to develop their knowledge and skills to get the best outcomes for all children, and putting measures in place to prevent the 'over-identification' of SEN in schools. The document emphasized the new focus on outcomes rather than processes in the identification of children with SEN and an assurance that 'pupils" needs are not 'missed'.

The Children and Families Act (2014), given royal assent in March 2014, legislated for a more inclusive approach in educational settings for children and young people with SEND. The vision for England outlined by the Act (2014) is a less fragmented, more 'joined-up' provision of children's services, where schools work closely with professionals from social, health and educational services. This vision calls for a more cooperative approach to management and leadership. By placing a duty on local authorities to identify all children in the area with SEND, it has brought greater urgency to educational settings in the early identification of need. The SEND Code of Practice 0-25 (DfE/DoH, 2015), legislated by Section 3 of the Children's and Families Act (2014), provides the guidance for practice. The Code of Practice is clear: for all those working with children with SEND and their families the following principles should underpin practice:

- take into account the views of children, young people and their families

- enable children, young people and their parents to participate in decision-making

- collaborate with partners in education, health and social care to provide support

- identify the needs of children and young people

- make high-quality provision to meet the needs of children and young people

- focus on inclusive practices and removing barriers to learning

- help children and young people to prepare for adulthood

(Source: adapted from: DfE, 2014: 6)

Since April 2011, schools in England have received Pupil Premium funding for pupils eligible for and claiming free school meals and those looked after by the state. Ofsted is clear: schools are accountable for the progress and attainment of these children and young people vulnerable to underachievement, with quantifiable outcomes. Government data highlights the intersection of characteristics shared by this group of learners; pupils claiming free school meals and those looked after by the state are more likely to be identified with SEND. In 2015, 61 per cent of the 69,540 Looked After Children in England had a special educational need (DfE, 2016). Recent research shows that children from low-income families are more likely to be born with an inherited SEND, are also more likely to develop SEND, and are less likely to move out of this category while at school than their more advantaged peers (Shaw et al., 2016). The particular focus of the Achievement for All programme has been very effective in supporting schools to maximize the outcomes for the most disadvantaged.

SEND: The Welsh context

Wales, on the other hand, has lagged slightly behind England in realizing its vision for SEND reform. In July 2015, the Welsh government published a draft called Additional Learning Needs Bill setting out a more inclusive approach for children and young people with special educational needs. The bill will be formally introduced into the legislative programme after the May 2016 Assembly elections. Proposals, including the introduction of a revised Code of Practice, will bring a new approach to the way children and young people with SEN are identified and assessed in Wales. The term 'Additional Learning Needs' (ALN) and 'Additional Learning Provision' (ALP) will replace Special Educational Needs and Special Educational Provision.

The new legislation will set out precise definitions to support educators and other professionals in the accurate, appropriate and timely identification of need. The proposals set out radical changes to the way support and services (education, health and social services) should be accessed by children and young people with SEN and ALN. In line with the Rights of Children and

Young Persons (Wales) Measure (WG, 2011), this includes provision for children and young people in schools and Further Education (FE) from birth to 25 years of age.

Currently, separate legislation exists for the FE provision and the term used for this age group is learning difficulties and/or disabilities (LDD) rather than SEN. Currently ALN is a non-statutory term used to define those children and young people who may require additional support or provision that is greater than that of their peers. This may be short or long term as a result of disability or home background circumstances as defined in Section 2 of the 2006 National Assembly for Wales Circular Inclusion and Pupil Support document. This fulfils the aims of the Children and Young People: Rights to Action (Welsh Assembly Government, 2004) agenda. SEN continues to be the statutory term used to define those children and young people who have severe, complex and/or specific learning difficulties as defined in the Education Act (1996) and the SEN Code of Practice for Wales (Welsh Assembly Government, 2004).

Proposed changes to the ALN provision in Wales have been influenced not only by the Children and Families Act (2014) and the SEN Code of Practice 0-25 (DfE/DoH, 2015) in England, but also by the Social Services and Well-being (Wales) Act 2014 and responses (in 2014) to the 2012 consultation document *Forward in Partnership for Children and Young People with Additional Needs* (WG, 2012).

The proposed changes are underpinned by an aspirational outlook on moving forward to a more inclusive approach in meeting the diverse needs of learners in Wales. This includes a focus on collaboration and outcomes, giving parents, carers, children and young people a 'voice' to influence what matters to them. Key principles that underpin the proposed ALN provision include the following:

- The best interests of learners must be a primary consideration.

- Learners' opinions should always be considered, along with those of their parents.

- Learners should expect to have their needs identified and met.

- Agreement on assessment and provision for learners should be simpler and less adversarial.

- Disagreements should be resolved as quickly and as easily as possible.

- All those involved in providing support to learners should work together to provide a seamless service.

(Welsh Government, 2014: 3–4)

These principles underpin the following proposals, which will impact on provision:

- replacing the statutory term 'Special Educational Needs' with 'Additional Learning Needs'

- introducing Individual Development Plans (IDP) to replace statements of SEN, non-statutory Individual Education Plans (IEPs) and post-16 assessments and plans

- having the Welsh government ministers publish a new Code of Practice for ALN

- setting out minimum requirements for what should be included within an IDP

- requiring local authorities to prepare an IDP and schools to implement provision outlined in and IDP for all children and young people including post-16 with ALN

- making sure that children, young people and their parents and carers have an active role in the IDP assessment and planning process from the outset through having their voice heard

- reviewing IDPs on an annual basis or earlier if needed

- providing guidance for professionals to ensure early identification of needs, even below compulsory school age

- having local authorities, local health boards and FE institutions to cooperate by sharing information in assessing, planning and delivering provision, thus promoting effective multi-agency collaboration

- having mainstream schools to designate an ALN coordinator to replace the SENCo

- having IDPs to replace Personal Education Plans (PEPs) for children looked after by the local authority

- having local authorities to put in place disagreement resolution arrangements and appoint an independent person to facilitate the resolution of disagreements

- giving the right of appeal to any child or young person who has an IDP (or their parent/carer) or those who believe they should have one.

In 2014, the Welsh government published *Qualified for life: An education improvement plan for 3 to 19 year olds in Wales*, which acknowledged the importance of a more inclusive approach to education in enabling every child to achieve their potential. The government's strategic priorities, set out in the document, are underpinned by a focus on literacy and numeracy and on breaking the link between disadvantage and poor educational attainment. The focus is clear: pupils, especially those who are disengaged or disadvantaged, should be supported by schools to enable them to fully access and enjoy equality of opportunity in learning. The SEN reforms are likely to go some way in enabling this vision to be realized.

Achievement for All: England and Wales

The Achievement for All Schools programme is designed to ensure that the schools are supported to meet the requirements as outlined in the SEND Code of Practice 0-25 (DfE/DoH, 2015) in England, the current SEN Code of Practice in Wales (WAG, 2002) and the Social Services and Well-being (Wales) Act 2014. The revised Code of Practice, published in England in 2014 reflects the 'key features' of the Achievement for All approach (TSO, 2013), with a strong focus on inclusive schooling. The programme has bridged three governments in England and continues to deliver high-quality, high-impact outcomes for vulnerable and disadvantaged pupils and those identified with SEND.

Education for All

The importance of education is something that is often lost on many of those compulsory school-age pupils participating in the process, particularly the lowest 20 per cent (or more) that do not attain even the basic level of literacy and numeracy needed to gain sustainable employment – a fundamental requirement for economic and social prosperity in this country. For many (but not all) of these pupils, the impact of their SEND or the social-economic context of their family is a lowering of aspiration by their teachers, parents, school leaders and wider professionals, resulting in limited access to learning and low attainment.

A lack of aspiration and access to learning and the subsequent impact on achievement underpins the education systems of England and Wales and is evidenced by the relatively high number of schools in their failure to address the needs of the disadvantaged (LAC and those eligible for FSM), those with SEND and others vulnerable to underachievement. In most schools this is unintended.

Schools annually celebrate examination results that exceed floor targets, boldly claiming significant success if the attainment of GCSE A–Cs or Key Stage 2 Level 4s exceeds the national average. There is rarely any mention or comment of the 20–30 per cent who have failed to reach the basic levels of literacy or numeracy. What are the life chances of the lowest 20 per cent?

Those that do not gain English and maths GCSE are higher in number in our prisons and drug centres and in premature deaths.

Digging deeper, the outcomes of the disadvantaged are equally challenging; the correlation between family income and special educational needs is over 70 per cent. The relationship between family income and low educational achievement has been discussed for generations. Grammar schools were seen to be an early solution in England, providing access to high levels of achievement for those considered to be academically able regardless of their socio-economic background. However, for those who fail their 11+, their home context impacts on their ability to progress on to further and higher education. In response to a perceived low academic attainment in local authority primary and secondary schools in England, Academies, Trusts and Free Schools were introduced, tasked with 'narrowing the gap', 'closing the gap' and 'raising standards'. Wales no longer has grammar schools and has resisted the introduction of academies, adhering to a community comprehensive model for all schools.

Irrespective of a school's structure, funding source or admissions policy, the Achievement for All framework focuses on the impact of teaching and learning on pupils. It supports high-quality teaching, good observation, planning and assessment, and appropriate interventions; this allows for timely and appropriate identification of any learning needs in children. Any concerns with children's learning can be addressed through a graduated approach – assess, plan, do and review, where evidence of progress is used to inform learning targets (DfE/DoH, 2015).

As educators, teachers and leaders of schools, there needs to be an awareness of the whole community in day-to-day practice. What are its values? What are the current tensions? What do teachers hope to achieve for children in their care? How can it be done in an inclusive way, that is, working both in and with the community? In order to answer these questions, educators must locate themselves as individuals within the community, becoming aware of their specific roles in helping the community to function inclusively and successfully.

Summary

Achievement for All takes a whole-school approach to school improvement, focused on improving teaching and learning for all pupils. The particular focus is on the 20 per cent of the school population identified as having SEND, those from socio-economic disadvantage, children looked after by the state and others vulnerable to underachievement. Too many of these pupils do not achieve as well as their peers relative to their starting points, and are leaving education without the skills and qualifications they need to become independent adults. Achievement for All is based on the belief that teachers and school leaders can have a profound impact on all pupils and young people by developing their Achievement, Access and Aspirations. This means having high expectations of what pupils can achieve, working in partnership with parents to set targets for learning and track progress, and increasing the range of learning opportunities available to them. While an effective teacher increases access and raises aspirations as a means to improving achievement, an inspirational teacher improves achievement in a way that changes pupils' aspirations, and in doing so improves their life chances by securing access to continued achievement and self-fulfilment.

A systemic change needs to occur in schools – in the classroom, in support teams and in leadership. Implementing Achievement for All practices builds confidence in raising the Achievement, Access and Aspirations of all learners. The impact is shared outcomes for all those at risk of underachievement and their parents through raising aspirations in every lesson. Confident school leaders and teachers raise the achievement of all pupils through the practice of Achievement for All, which is transferable to learning throughout the school. The Achievement for All programme is delivered through coaching and online support provided in English and Welsh – The Bubble – with over 2,000 tools, curriculum and assessment plans, research summaries and case studies that provide bespoke support, information, guidance and self-evaluation practice for leaders, teachers, parents and carers.

Since the pilot in 2009, the impact of the Achievement for All programme on improving outcomes for children and young people has been profound as illustrated by a range of independent research reports (University of Manchester, 2011), PwC (2014, 2015, 2016). The following chapter provides a more in-depth analysis of the impact of the programme in England and Wales.

CHAPTER FOUR

The Achievement for All Programme

The aspirations and achievements of all of our children and young people, both in school and in the wider society, are important to us all – whether we are parents, leaders, teachers, policy makers or employers. As you have read, Achievement for All is a programme that focuses on improving the Aspirations, Access and Achievement of pupils with Special Educational Needs and Disabilities (SEND), Looked After Children, those from socio-economic disadvantage and others vulnerable to underperformance. In England, this represents around 20 per cent of pupils. The programme is based on the belief that school leaders, teachers, teaching assistants support staff can have a profound impact on all children by raising their aspirations and achievements and improving their access to learning. This is a strong contributory factor in why the programme has been independently shown to make the most of the ability and potential of *all* young people.

In March 2014, the Welsh government agreed to provide funding to support the development and roll-out of the Achievement for All programme in Wales. The Welsh government wanted the programme to help schools in three ways: provide evidence for the effective use of the Pupil Deprivation grant; help them prepare for nationally established Estyn inspections (similar to Ofsted in England); and bring together national, local and school-based interventions under one, single, effective framework. On this basis Achievement for All and the Regional Consortia agreed to initiate an Achievement for All Pathfinder programme beginning in January 2014 and continuing until December 2014 with the expectation that the schools involved would continue with the programme for at least a year after completion. The fourteen Pathfinder schools were located in local authorities that make up the Central South Consortium (Bridgend, Cardiff, Merthyr Tydfil, Rhondda Cynon Taff and the Vale of Glamorgan); 479 learners participated in the programme. The programme was implemented and developed in the Pathfinder schools in Wales in a similar way to that which is done in England, with the exception of differing tailored modules which included: The Curriculum Cymreig and Community Engagement and Partnership Working. Achievement for All made documents available in both English and Welsh, fully contextualizing them to take into account the different policy landscape in Wales. This chapter will consider the implementation and development of the Achievement for All programme in schools in England and the adapted programme for Wales. It considers the four key, interdependent elements of the programme (Leadership, Teaching and Learning, Parent and Carer Engagement and Wider Outcomes and Opportunities) and how the framework they provide enables schools to apply Aspiration, Access and Achievement to all pupils.

Element 1: Leadership

In March 2011, the National College published the findings of a two-year study involving 220 head teachers in focus groups and surveys, which considered leadership in the context of the Achievement for All programme. School leaders agreed that vision, commitment, collaboration and communication were critical to the successful impact of Achievement for All. The leadership element was further developed to ensure that participating schools keep a sharp focus on the Achievement, Access and Aspirations of pupils identified with SEND and others vulnerable to underperformance. The key elements of leadership are:

- **Vision** – A set of core values and beliefs, centred on high expectations for all pupils and positive engagement with parents, staff and other professionals. A wide range of learning opportunities are on offer to the pupils.

- **Commitment** – A commitment to core values, whereby appropriate opportunities are secured and provided to all pupils, and their progress is tracked. Staff development is supported and promoted.

- **Collaboration** – A culture of collaboration between staff, parents and other organizations. Leaders in and across schools/academies work together with a sense of collective responsibility.

- **Communication** – An ability to communicate effectively with all staff, parents, pupils and external agencies, enabling the school community to share in the vision.

These four characteristics define effective inclusive leadership as determined by Achievement for All. They are manifested in practice in the flowing ways:

Vision

Vision becomes apparent in both informal and formal communications – staff meetings, conversations in corridors, meetings with parents and other agencies. Effective leaders are reflective thinkers, who are constantly evaluating, questioning and challenging current school practices and culture. They embed their belief that ALL children can achieve and make progress constantly. They are able to demonstrate

- a core moral purpose.
- consistent message and role-modelling.
- knowledge and context of community.
- accountability and responsibility.
- self-awareness and the ability to reflect.
- risk-taking and innovation.

Commitment

Successful leaders reflect their commitment to their pupils through their behaviours as leaders and managers. They are relentless in securing the most appropriate provision. They commit to providing high-quality resources and engage specialist staff where appropriate. They invest in ensuring that effective strategies and systems are in place to track pupils' progress. They have a strategic view of what is needed to skill their workforce to improve inclusion, are committed to constant development of staff and successfully deploy appropriate staff to meet the needs of the individual. They ensure that time is committed in staff meetings and elsewhere to discussion and dialogue about improving provision for vulnerable pupils. They value the engagement with parents by committing time and resources to ensure that effective structured conversations can take place within and outside the school day. Above all, they secure the commitment of all staff and ensure that their commitment is underpinned by a sense of collective responsibility for the achievement of all pupils (NCSL, 2011).

Collaboration

Successful provision to ensure that pupils identified with SEND progress and achieve wider outcomes requires a culture of collaboration – with and between staff, with parents and with other agencies. Effective collaboration relies on leaders in and across schools working together with a sense of collective responsibility for vulnerable learners and pupils identified with SEND. It also means that leaders are outward facing – they look beyond their own school, they show an appreciation and understanding that all schools are different, and that strengths and good practice can be shared. Effective leaders' model shared working practices in school and between schools and phases of education. In the successful schools within the Achievement for All projects, leadership is both a collaborative and distributed activity (NCSL, 2011).

Communication

The successful leadership of SEND relies on effective communications at a range of levels – with pupils; with parents and carers; with staff in and between schools and other services/agencies. Successful leaders are good at engaging others. They nurture relationships with pupils and their parents or carers. They are good listeners and can demonstrate that they value the contribution of others. They invest time in communicating with parents.

Effective leaders articulate and communicate a vision, which they encourage others to share and develop. They actively encourage formal and informal dialogue about strategies to improve the Achievement for All pupils. They share information about pupils' attainment and progress and celebrate achievement. Through their communications they give value to wider outcomes as well as those reported in performance tables (NCSL, 2011).

Schools that have demonstrated vision, commitment, communication and collaboration have seen a significant impact on the progress of pupils identified with SEND by focusing on: assessment, tracking and intervention, structured conversations and parental engagement and improving wider outcomes and opportunities. Effective leadership is of vital importance to ensuring the positive impact of Achievement for All.

Element 2: Teaching and learning

High-quality teaching and learning supports schools to improve the attainment and progress of students with SEND, Looked After Children and others vulnerable to underperformance. Its implementation is centred on the key areas of assessment, data tracking and target setting. In essence when there is a rigorous, high-quality approach to these areas the attainment and progress of children and young people is significantly improved.

Developing this type of approach across the school is based on teachers, pupils and their parents knowing where the children are in their learning, where they are aiming to get and how to get there. It is founded on collaborative working and active learning. For schools, this means having good policies for marking and feedback, strong whole-school assessment systems in place and good monitoring and evaluation approaches to processes and practices. For teachers, it means knowing the pupils and how they learn, having high aspirations for their learning, giving children a sense of ownership of learning, taking a more personalized approach to children's learning and keeping good records. For pupils, it means being able to access the curriculum, raising their aspirations and increasing their achievements. Access will be closely connected to their own feelings of confidence: confidence in their competencies, high self-esteem and self-mastery skills. For parents, it means knowing where their child is in their learning, knowing how to support them in their learning and having high aspirations for their learning and achievement.

A key feature of the Achievement for All programme is the way the framework enables schools to give teachers responsibility for the pupils in their classroom. In schools, this is led by senior leadership teams and supported through focused staff training. It is reflected in the following:

- teachers taking a more active role in the assessment and monitoring of pupils with SEND

- structured conversations with parents (three per year as determined by pupil needs between key teacher, parents and their child), enabling teachers and parents to work together to change their own and parents' expectations of pupils with SEND and recognize pupils' potential

- changing teacher knowledge and understanding of pupils with SEND, resulting in a more personalized approach to teaching and learning within the classroom

- teachers seeing CPD and other training opportunities provided through Achievement for All and generally associated with structured conversations as very helpful and applying them in their daily interactions with other staff members and parents

- in schools/academies with increased pupil attainment and other improved outcomes, teachers being more frequently involved in reviewing individual pupil targets

- data-led discussions between SLT and class teachers, providing opportunity to identify pupils not making the expected progress and to find appropriate interventions to help them

- teachers planning together for differentiation, allowing for greater focus on individual pupils.

(Adapted from Humphrey and Squires, 2011)

Evidence from the Achievement for All programme has shown that teacher development is implicit in the framework. The shift in teacher attitude to teaching and their development of more inclusive practices through the Achievement for All framework – as a result of a greater focus on identification of pupils at risk of underperformance, their needs, assessment and provision – supports and encourages raised teacher aspirations and expectations for all children. Through the structured conversations with parents, teachers become more aware of and develop a greater understanding of their pupils' needs and potential. This contributes to an increased sense of professional responsibility and ownership in the classroom. The greater focus on the learning and development of children and young people with SEND and other vulnerable groups, along with training and guidance leads to more effective teacher approaches in pedagogical practice. In particular, practices become more inclusive, enabling teachers to more effectively meet the diverse needs of all pupils. In essence, through the Achievement for All framework, with focused training, what was previously considered to be an extra practice becomes rooted in everyday practice.

Element 3: Parent and carer engagement: The structured conversation

Parent and carer engagement is at the centre of the Achievement for All framework. Structured conversations between parents or carers and teachers have improved parental engagement with the school and their involvement in their child's learning and achievement. Evidence from the programme shows that the particular open dialogue approach – developed through a series of three structured conversations between key teachers and parents and, if appropriate, their children – provides a platform from which parents can effectively engage in the learning process. Based on the idea of giving parents and carers of children with SEND and others vulnerable to underachievement the opportunity to discuss their aspirations for their children, Achievement for All provides schools with a framework to do this better. This element of the programme has had a significant impact on pupils and parents, changing families' lives and enhancing life chances.

Founded on open channels of communication with parents and carers, structured conversations enable schools to focus on three things:

- How best to contact parents and, in some cases, remove communication barriers.
- How to align the structured conversations to target setting.
- How to engage children better in their learning.

The following case study provides an example of how increased parental engagement had a positive impact on children's outcomes.

Case study: The Meads Primary School

Context

The Meads Primary School is a recently expanded large primary school in north Luton, Bedfordshire with 520 pupils. It was rated as 'Good' at its last Ofsted inspection in November 2011. The school joined the Achievement for All schools programme in September 2012 to improve outcomes for children with SEND, those from poor families and others vulnerable to underachievement; the school part-funded the programme by using the Pupil Premium grant. The Meads is a value-based school and shares the Achievement for All values, which are literally painted on corridor walls.

Approach

The SLT's vision of high expectations for all children including SEND and vulnerable groups was shared with staff, with the responsibility of progress of these groups firmly placed with class teachers. This vision was reinforced from the start of the academic year through the delivery of Achievement for All training for all staff. The school champion recognized that sharing her vision of Achievement for All through an action plan would be a major driving force for its success and so incorporated it into the SDP.

An Achievement for All governor was established and regular reports were given to the governing body. Achievement for All was a standing item on staff meetings and SLT agendas. The profile of the target children was raised with staff. The progress of individual children was discussed at staff briefings every week, and photographs of the children added to the staffroom noticeboard – staff were encouraged to congratulate them on their hard work.

An audit of parental engagement of the target groups was conducted and revealed that many did not engage fully. All staff involved directly with the target groups, together with family workers, received Structured Conversation training. A guidance book tailored to The Meads Primary School was produced providing checklists for staff when organizing structured conversations. Staff initially encountered difficulties engaging some parents but were persistent and offered a wide variety of times as well as a crèche to overcome barriers to attendance.

Prior to the structured conversations, parents were invited to a parent information meeting where they were given a summary of Achievement for All, and were able to discuss what to expect in the meetings. Parents were given a book that would form the basis of the conversation, to complete the section about their child prior to the meeting.

By the end of the year, every class teacher had carried out structured conversations, and some extended the principle to any child within their class where they felt there would be benefit. After the first round of structured conversations, teachers were overwhelmingly positive about the insight they gave into each child, and looked at ways to further improve the experience.

Impact

- Parental engagement for children identified with SEND rose from 55 per cent at green to 100 per cent at green by term 3.
- Parental engagement for children from socio-economic disadvantaged families rose from 0 per cent at green to 100 per cent at green by term 3.
- Target pupils from socio-economic disadvantage made 4.8 points progress over three terms, and those with SEN made 3.7 points of progress.

Key learning

- Structured Conversations foster a trusting relationship: parents feel able to speak openly and teachers gain a greater insight into a child's life.
- It was important to prepare parents so that they could be confident when it came to the Structured Conversation meeting.
- It is essential that a member of the SLT drives the programme through rigorous monitoring and coaching.

For parents, structured conversations provide a forum to engage with their child's school, speak about their child's interests and learning, and their aspirations for their child. It is an opportunity to enhance and further develop their aspirations and to communicate this to their child. For schools, structured conversations provide time to listen to parents, talk to parents about their children's learning and reflect upon ways to transfer this to the classroom.

The effectiveness of this approach is reflected in the following comments made by parents of children who participated in the programme:

I feel listened to and really valued in the structured conversations. (Year 5 parent)

I know exactly what type of support my son is receiving and what his targets are so that I can help him more too. (Year 5 parent)

My son is now more confident, he interacts better, he is learning more and he feels better about himself. He used to really struggle and was so clingy with me. (Year 1 parent)

Wider outcomes and opportunities

Evidence from Achievement for All shows that before schools joined the programme, children and young people with SEND were less likely to access extracurricular opportunities provided by schools than their peers (Humphrey and Squires, 2011). This is also supported by the wider literature; in the United States, Carter (2010) highlights the opportunities missed by high-school students with disabilities (this includes building relationships with peers and developing leadership skills) because they do not access the wider provision.

In many schools in England, wider provision is often seen as an 'add-on' to the main curriculum and can be relatively underdeveloped. This was supported by the Ofsted report *Learning Outside the Classroom* (2008), which highlighted the variability in all aspects of provision. Where provision was 'good', the report provided strong evidence for greater engagement of children in their learning, their higher achievement and better well-being, when they are involved in extracurricular activities. However, for maximum benefit, the report highlighted the need for activities to be an integral part of the curriculum, planned to support other learning and well evaluated. This also reflects element four of the Achievement for All approach, where schools work with the achievement coach to identify, plan and integrate wider provision for children with SEND, Looked After Children, those eligible for Free School Meals and other vulnerable learners. Evidence from both the Achievement for All pilot (Humphrey and Squires, 2011) and the national roll-out of the programme has shown the benefits of wider provision across schools. The following case study illustrates the impact of the Achievement for All programme, with particular emphasis on widening outcomes and opportunities.

Case study: Frederick Bird Primary School, Coventry

Context

Frederick Bird is a mixed-community primary school in the centre of Coventry. It has 673 on roll, where 76.7 per cent of the pupils are EAL, 13.5 per cent have been identified as SEND and 40.3 per cent are eligible for Free School Meals. It aims to become a four-form entry school by September 2018. Forty-six languages are spoken and fifteen translators work alongside the pupils. The school wanted to provide some wider outcomes for fifteen pupils in Year 5 with 'School Action Plus' status. Many of the children had attendance issues and struggled to show their capabilities on 'in school' tasks. Many of the children had no opportunities to attend after-school clubs or any sporting opportunities in the community. The issues they presented were often complex: speech and language/communication problems, learning difficulties, attachment disorder, mental health difficulties, behaviour challenges, attendance issues and personal hygiene concerns. Pupils were from many of the 'vulnerable' groups in school, Bengali pupils, White British boys and Gypsy Roma families.

Approach

The school planned a year-long project called 'AfA Active'. Six sporting opportunities were provided during the academic year. The project is still continuing. Every half-term a sporting opportunity is provided on a Saturday morning for the Achievement for All cohorts. The school began with cycling. It was able to use the large school site for the first part of the project. During the morning of the activity the school also provided drinks and snacks or a 'second breakfast'. In the first half-term the children achieved their bronze cycling proficiency. Some of the children began the project without being able to ride a bike at all. As an additional unplanned outcome some the Achievement for All parents had individual adult cycling lessons and learnt to ride a bike themselves.

The next opportunity was rambling and orienteering. The school minibus was used to visit sites around Coventry and the West Midlands. Children were taught mapping, rambling and orienteering skills and visited a variety of sites including Oxford Canal and the Burton Dassett Hills. Next was swimming and the children achieved their Level 3 British Swimming Association awards. The children then worked on Basic Life Saving to obtain the 'Rookie Lifeguard' qualification. Other activities include rock climbing, canoeing and sailing.

Outcomes

The school employed specialist teachers for many of the sports and this helped raise the standard of achievement. It introduced independence as a key skill to be practised and taught. It is considered important to have the same members of school staff to support the project, as families can build relationships with those staff and trust staff. There is obviously the addition of specialist teachers who can be different.

Impact

Overall, children's attendance and attitude to learning improved. There was a marked improvement in their attitude to school, and relationships with adults improved. The children worked more readily in teams together and had something important in common. They were more confident to take part in sports in school and are supported by their Achievement for All friends when they do.

Pupils felt confident to suggest to their families that they all take part in a physical activity out of school. Families developed closer relationships with staff and generally were much more positive about what their children could achieve if given the opportunity.

Through Achievement for All, participation in school clubs and activities is encouraged as a means of developing self-esteem and the skills needed to work with others. Many Achievement for All schools have considered what is available for all pupils, an outcome has been the creation of a programme of fully inclusive activities. This supports the participation, enjoyment and achievement of pupils in all elements of school life. Element four of the Achievement for All framework aims to support the participation and enjoyment of pupils in all elements of school life; evaluation of the effectiveness of this element is centred on pupil well-being. Evidence shows that poor pupil well-being is often reflected in their attendance, behaviour and relationships with others at school. The 2015 Children's Society Report found that children who were repeatedly bullied (that is, more than four times in the last three months) were significantly more likely to experience low well-being (37 per cent) than those that had never been bullied (6 per cent). Sadly, these indicators also have a negative impact on children's engagement with learning, attainment and progress. Founded on an evidence base of what works for children in the area of improving their wider outcomes, Achievement for All developed a framework for schools to effectively implement and develop this element of the programme. Schools can expect the following outcomes:

- improved attendance
- barriers to participation removed
- improved behaviour (children develop strategies to regulate their emotions)
- children with greater resilience and self-esteem
- developing positive relationships with others
- increasing participation in all aspects of the school and the community
- including participation in extracurricular activities.

Achievement for All: Measuring impact

Implemented at the school level and focusing on aspects of teaching/teacher quality, the programme enables teacher development, without focusing on individual teacher performance. Monitoring and evaluation are critical to the successful implementation and development of the Achievement for All programme and 3As principles within the school. Having implemented the Achievement for All framework, school champions and achievement coaches will need to monitor its progress in collaboration with leaders, teachers, parents, pupils and wider professionals. Monitoring will also enable leaders and teachers to obtain the best results from the available resources. Most significantly, monitoring will enable staff to reflect on their own practice, an outcome of which is enhanced job satisfaction (Humphrey and Squires, 2011).

Within the Achievement for All framework a range of qualitative and quantitative data will be shared with the achievement coach, so that, together, the school champion and achievement coach can make judgements about the impact of the framework on pupil progress and achievement across academic and wider outcomes and also the impact on the engagement of parents and carers. The achievement coach and school champion will look at termly progress data for reading, writing, maths, behaviour and attendance. This data will be used to evaluate the impact of the framework on academic progress. Data analysis of groups will identify the impact on progress across wider outcomes and the extent to which the framework has succeeded in its overall aims.

In the first stage of implementing the Achievement for All framework, the school champion (member of the school leadership team), in collaboration with their SLT and the achievement coach, will carry out a needs analysis to determine the school's priorities at the beginning of the school's Achievement for All journey and to plan the route towards achieving the Quality Mark an external assessment of standards achieved. The needs analysis is based on Achievement for All Quality Standards, which are the processes that schools embed in order to achieve the accelerated progress necessary to meet the Quality Mark criteria. The needs analysis is a self-evaluation by the school against the Quality Standards, designed to be a dynamic document that will be revisited regularly throughout the two years of the Achievement for All programme. The needs analysis is completed during the achievement coach's early visits and schools are asked to give consideration to their judgements in preparation for this meeting. The needs analysis will support:

- overall planning and implementation of the framework; specifically, the activities that the achievement coach will lead over the following sequence of visits
- identification of areas of focus for element four (wider outcomes)
- identification of any staff professional development needs
- monitoring of the impact of the framework by establishing a baseline position.

The Achievement for All regional leads and achievement leads carry out joint visits to schools with achievement coaches to monitor the progress of Achievement for All and to gather feedback on the framework as a whole. Schools are also sent twice-yearly school champion surveys, to gain feedback on how schools feel about the impact of the programme and how we can improve the framework.

External evaluations of the impact of the Achievement for All programme have been carried out by the University of Manchester (2009–11 and 2016–19), PwC (2011–16) and by the National College of Teaching and Leadership (2014–15). The NCTL evaluation determined that 'existing teaching school practice may also be better than the first year of AfA with regard to the exposure of free school meals (FSM) pupils to this treatment' (NCTL, 2016). The majority of the thirty schools cited in the NCTL study had engaged with the programme for two terms. An aim of the programme is to work with the lowest achieving 20 per cent of FSM and SEND pupils; not all FSM pupils will fall into this category. This finding emphasizes the need for leaders and teachers to adopt the Achievement for All programme over two years and to commit to improving progress of the lowest achieving 20 per cent of pupils.

Summary

A systemic change needs to occur in schools – in the classroom, in support teams and in leadership. Implementing Achievement for All practices builds confidence in raising the achievement, access and aspirations of all learners. The impact is shared outcomes for all children and young people vulnerable to underperformance and their parents through raising aspirations in every lesson. Confident school leaders and teachers raise the achievement of all pupils through the practice of Achievement for All, which is transferable to learning throughout the school. The outcome is achievement for all and, for those who are driven by examination results, the possibility of 100 per cent success.

Impact on progress is a key driver for the Achievement for All coaches. Data is gathered on a termly basis to provide a summary of outcomes for every targeted pupil (average thirty-nine targeted pupils per school) in reading, writing and maths. The gathering of data is discussed in detail by the coach with the school champion, thus providing a mechanism by which each pupil, teacher, parent and leader can monitor and adapt practice on a regular basis; evidence informed. The following chapter provides a summary of the impact of the programme as validated by PwC.

CHAPTER FIVE

The Impact of Achievement for All in England and Wales

Achievement for All is guided by the Theory of Change (ToC) developed by PwC in consultation with the DfE and Achievement for All, which demonstrates how its activities are expected to translate into outcomes. The ToC is supported by a literature review, which is revisited and updated annually. Evidence shows that the wider body of knowledge supports the aims of Achievement for All. In addition, the research evidence continues to uphold the close link between the activities and outcomes of the schools.

In both England and Wales, there is evidence that the Achievement for All programme is making a difference to the lives of disadvantaged children and young people. Independent social impact assessment reports show that in England the programme is having a significant impact in closing the gap in reading, writing and maths for pupils identified with SEND, those from socio-economic disadvantage and others vulnerable to underachievement (PwC, 2013, 2014, 2015). In Wales, after one year of the Pathfinder programme, findings were equally positive. Children and young people participating in the programme made good progress; this was reflected in improved attendance, fewer incidents of poor behaviour and improvements in reading levels. Because of the relatively large sample of participating primary schools, data from primary schools was statistically significant. This chapter looks at the impact of the Achievement for All programme on schools in England and Wales.

To date, beneficiaries of the programme in England include 3,760 schools/settings, 1,767,100 pupils (indirect), 172,111 target pupils (direct), 252,238 parents and carers, 69,197 teachers, 12,879 school leaders and 29,650 wider professionals (PwC, 2015). In Wales, fourteen schools and settings (four secondary schools, a special education centre, a special school and eight primary schools) benefitted from the programme, along with 479 pupils (direct). The first part of the chapter considers findings from the programme in England. These are based on the most recent Social Impact Assessment (PwC, 2015), which focused on assessing the impact of the programme over time, on the attainment and aspirations of targeted pupils, and on wider outcomes for all those benefitting from it. These are presented as a series of case studies. The second part of the chapter considers findings from Wales, based on an independent evaluation of the Pathfinder programme by the Wales Centre for Equity in Education (2015) (a joint initiative between the University of Wales and the University of Wales Trinity Saint David).

England: Overview

Findings from the Social Impact Assessment (PwC, 2015) showed that schools involved in Achievement for All exceeded national attainment targets, with overall average increases in APS of 4.8 (reading), 4.6 (writing) and 4.4 (maths) being reported through the termly data, up to 55 per cent above national expectations in reading at KS3–4 and up to 40 per cent above national expectations for all pupils across reading, writing and maths. Findings from parents were also positive; 80 per cent of parents, whose child was participating in the programme, reported that their child was improving in each subject. In addition, pupil progress data from autumn 2013 and spring 2015 pointed to an ongoing impact on attainment across all subjects, with 75 per cent of pupils believing that they can now get better marks at school. Schools also reported an increase in pupil confidence and aspiration since joining the programme, with pupil feedback highlighting a positive impact on their social and behavioural outcomes. In addition, Achievement for All is supporting the implementation of the SEN Code of Practice 0-25 (DfE/DoH, 2015). Overall findings show that Achievement for All is having a positive impact on aspirations and attitudes and in creating better life chances and improved future prospects for pupils involved in the programme (PwC, 2015) as shown in Table 5.1.

Table 5.1 England: Impact on pupil attainment

Outcomes as identified in the Theory of Change	Detail of outcomes
Attainment	• Accelerated progression and attainment • Increased post-16 participation • Better socialization for work
Aspiration	• Increased aspirations and positive attitude • Better life chances and improved future prospects
Wider Outcomes	• Improved attendance • Less difficulty making friends • Improved social and behavioural outcomes

The best thing about (Achievement for All) for me, as a parent, was being able to pinpoint the areas where P needed the most help – for example, in reading and English language, and some maths topics.

(Source: PwC, 2015, parent survey)

I've been doing better at school, and now I communicate more with teachers.

(Source: PwC, 2015, pupil survey)

Evidence shows that Achievement for All is meeting its aim of accelerated pupil progress. For those participating in the programme, their improvement in reading, writing and maths exceeded the national measures of expected progress. Pupils involved in the programme for a second year said they enjoyed reading, writing and maths more than before they joined and more than in the previous year of the programme. In addition, parents involved with the programme for longer periods of time were more positive about its impact on their children than those more recent participants. This suggested that the impact of Achievement for All increases over time. The following case study shows how Achievement for All is contributing to better attainment and in the following example, the outcome focuses on better socialization for work.

Case study – attainment: Better socialization for work

'Throughout his years at school, R had achieved well below the age expected levels for his year group and progress was very poor in all areas of the curriculum.'

(School head teacher)

Background

R is a primary school pupil who was in Year 4 when he began Achievement for All. He has now transitioned to secondary school. When R joined the school, he was immediately part of the target group. The focus for him was aspirations and progress. The school explored his interests and used these to 'hook him into the learning'. For him, this took a little while and the turning point was getting his Mum involved. His mother was invited to a regular SEN review that term, during which some of the time was used to talk about what the school was trying to do to motivate R more. She was really interested and she was asked to talk to him about it at home. A further date was to meet again to discuss how it was going.

Achievement for All school intervention

The school set the target group a challenge to come up with an idea for a product to sell at the Summer Fayre. The children were paired up (for support) and given time to do some research. The emphasis was on talking; asking questions and listening to the responses. If they could remember the responses, then verbal feedback was fine. All of the children returned from their research and you could almost touch the enthusiasm in the room. They were bursting with ideas and couldn't wait to tell the teacher. When the teacher talked 1:1 with R, he said that he enjoyed the groups more than when he was in class because often he found writing really hard and sometimes the work was tricky. He couldn't always remember what he was doing and his friends wouldn't always be able to help him. He didn't like having an adult helping him because his friends would see and might make fun of him. R's teacher began to notice his growing enthusiasm, and she began to plan his work to link in as much as possible with his interests. This meant he was participating more in lessons and beginning to make progress. It wasn't large steps of progress, but for R it was progress and it hadn't happened for a long time. R remained part of the target group until he left the school at the end of Year 6. He is now in Year 7 at a specialist secondary school within the locality.

Impact

'R participates in lots of outdoor and school sports activities. At primary school, he would not participate in sports or after school activities. He now swims once a week and attends Youth Club twice weekly. He also attends a shadow boxing club once a week and is currently looking to begin learning Karate. R is making good progress in his new school, and is continuing to learn key life skills to equip him as an adult, but also to prepare him for a life in employment. He talks happily about how happy he is and how much he enjoys school. He sleeps all night now and Mum has even taken him and his siblings camping in the school holidays.'

(School Champion)

England: Impact on pupil aspirations

'Pupils are being listened to and have opportunity to express their aspirations more clearly. They are given more one-to-one time with their teacher.'

(Source: PwC, 2015 School Champion survey)

'(The best thing for me has been) seeing my son come out of his shell – he's so much more confident now.'

(Source: PwC, 2015 parent survey)

'If I needed help in a lesson I feel like I can tell someone now.'

(Source: PwC, 2015 pupil survey)

Findings showed that school champions were positive about the impact on pupil confidence and aspiration, and on teachers' own aspirations for their pupils; 75 per cent of pupils felt more confident in their own ability to achieve better marks. The following case study shows how Achievement for All is contributing to increased aspirations and a more positive attitude.

Case study – pupil aspirations: Increased aspirations and positive attitude

'When asked what E enjoyed at school, Mum said her child enjoyed doing "nothing" at school. She was happy to come but wasn't progressing.'

(Mum of Year 5 pupil E)

Background

E is a Year 5 primary school pupil who was very quiet and unassuming and shy when she joined the programme. There was no troublesome behaviour but she was making no progress. E's parent is a single Mum and while there were no real issues in the family, her Mum was very concerned that she was not making any headway in school.

Achievement for All school intervention

The school started involving E with a sewing afternoon where a parent or family member was invited along to get involved. E's grandma came in. They designed a costume together and went on to be involved in some fashion shows. This was the start of the breakthrough with E. From the Fashion Show, her confidence just grew, and then from that she joined the drama club, and the choir, which took her to some outside events, which was a completely new experience. Being able to do this really boosted her confidence. She has also been involved in cheerleading which she never would have done.

Impact

'We are now beginning to see confidence in terms of E's ability to speak out in class which is a massive achievement in a short time. Mum is now willing to have extra work sent home and support her daughter in whatever way she can. She comes in for every meeting and now feels welcome in the school.'

(School Champion)

Wider outcomes and opportunities

'I'm glad I'm getting helped more, and I'm happier at school now.'

(Source: PwC, 2015 pupil survey)

Evidence from the 2015 surveys of the school champions, parents, and pupils show that Achievement for All is having an impact on social and behavioural outcomes. Findings also suggested that Achievement for All has a positive impact across attendance, behaviour, extracurricular activities, and parent and pupil engagement.

In addition, the longer a school is involved in Achievement for All, the stronger the impact on wider outcomes. In addition, pupils report improvements in their enjoyment of lessons, their behaviour, and their wish to go to school. The following case study shows how Achievement for All is contributing to wider outcomes, where the focus is improved attendance.

Case study – wider outcomes: Improved attendance

'M's attendance was shocking at 81%, but Dad just wouldn't come into the school to see me.'

(Head teacher)

Background

M is a Year 3 pupil whose attendance was poor and was compounded by a lack of parental engagement with the school. The school kept sending out letters to Dad asking him to come into the school, and the head teacher would get no response. The head teacher eventually got Dad into a structured conversation where the teaching staff were able to focus on the Achievement for All elements with him.

Achievement for All structured conversation

During the structured conversation with Dad, the school discovered that dyslexia was running throughout the family and that Dad had been scared and bullied at school, and had got into lots of trouble. He couldn't read or write and he said he didn't want that for his son. The school began to build a relationship with Dad and to encourage good attendance. M began to attend after-school activities. As a result of the contact with the parent, a dyslexic screening check was carried out on M and the school was also able to put other things in place as a result of that conversation.

Impact

M's attendance has increased from 81 per cent to 89 per cent. At the start of the programme, M was working well below his age-related expectations. Now he is closing the gap with his peers, and by the end of this academic year, he will be only slightly below age-related expectations.

'Because his attendance has now come up, as a result his academic attainment has improved. He now attends extracurricular activities and is entering into school life whole-heartedly. Dad now knows that I will do my best for him.'

(Head teacher)

Wales: Impact on leadership

The schools in Wales showed a similar pattern to that in England. The programme developed most effectively when the head teacher was very involved and proactive. In most schools this was the case and in a few they were at the forefront of driving the programme forward and planning how best to extend it during 2015. Initial implementation varied between schools; in some schools staff were more involved at the outset and in others less so. Where the programme developed well, senior school leaders took a particular interest and supported colleagues in the management of the programme by providing appropriate time and resources.

The School Champion worked closely with the Achievement coach to identify priorities and monitor progress. The programme had a whole-school profile.

Schools valued the support of the Achievement for All coaches. They regarded the coaches as helpful, highly professional and very accessible, valuing the termly review and the resultant action planning with the coach; schools generally saw this as an additional and very useful element of their self-evaluation and forward thinking.

The extent to which the Special Needs/Additional Learning Needs coordinators (SENCOs/ALNCOs) were involved in the programme varied considerably. A few schools appointed link governors. In most cases the Achievement for All agenda was included in schools' strategic planning although such links were not always explicit.

Similarly, the extent to which the Consortium Challenge Advisers were involved in considering the programme and its impact on schools they are responsible for was limited.

Overall, head teachers valued the programme but recognized that it is demanding in relation to the time, including staff time, that is required for successful delivery. However, evidence from Achievement for All's experience in England and early development in Wales demonstrates the value that it can add if schools are prepared to commit resources, including staff time, to its delivery.

Wales: Impact on teaching and learning

Teachers of target group pupils felt they gained new skills and expertise in developing finely tuned and precise next steps for pupils around shared goals. In such cases Achievement for All enabled a strong partnership to develop between the teacher, pupil and parent or carer.

In building up a comprehensive picture of how the programme is impacting on pupil progress at individual and school level, baseline data is collected on each of the target group pupils at the start of the programme and each term. In England, figures for schools working with Achievement for All in 2013/14 year indicated, that based on a weighted average of APS data, schools involved in the programme for a minimum of three terms had increased APS in reading by 5.2 points, in writing by 4.9 points and in maths by 4.8 points. In Wales, when interpreting the data, it was important to bear in mind that the sample – particularly of secondary schools – was small and the data comprised aggregated averages which inevitably masked some excellent examples of individual pupil progress. At the end of the first year of the programme in Wales, only primary data had some statistical significance because of the larger number of schools involved. This showed that the APS increased over three terms by 5.19 points in reading, 5.61 points in writing and 5.16 points in mathematics. This compared favourably with England.

There was also widespread agreement among teachers that the programme was contributing to improvements in learning. Furthermore, even where target groups made more modest gains, the schools believed the rates of improvement would strengthen as the programme was further embedded over the two years it takes to fully implement actions and activities that are known to impact positively on pupil outcomes.

One of the important gains for teachers was their development of greater knowledge of pupils' all-round development, particularly at home; this tended to follow on from the structured conversations with parents and carers. Like England, this increased knowledge helped teachers to tailor their classroom approaches to become more inclusive. In addition, a few teachers believed that the programme had improved their self-evaluation skills and awareness of data to inform planning for improvement. They continued throughout the programme to fine-tune their assessment skills in developing shared goals with pupils. Although still largely underdeveloped by the end of the first year, 'the voice of learners' was becoming much more of a feature in the schools where the programme was developing well.

Wales: Impact on parent and carer engagement

Across schools, the programme's greatest impact was in the area of increased parent and carer engagement. Schools attributed this to the particular use of and approach of the structured conversations. There was general agreement among teachers and senior leaders that the structured conversation training provided by the Achievement for All coaches was good quality and very useful. Champions were asked to rate parental engagement (on a basic red, amber and green (RAG) scale) before the programme began and at the end of each term. Data from primary schools suggested that parental engagement increased from around one in five before the programme began to three in five at the end of the first year.

The meetings between teachers and parents and carers usually lasted between thirty and forty-five minutes; in some cases, they lasted for one hour. There was a strong indication that the structured conversations had a considerable influence on the approaches taken by those teachers responsible for target group pupils. In the main this stemmed from the structured conversations giving teachers a much fuller picture of pupils and parents and carers. In turn this generated mutually agreed realistic, but ambitious, targets. These were backed up by clearly defined actions and precise next steps. In a few schools this is also said to be both influencing assessment and planning interventions, not only with target groups, but also with other pupils in the class. In addition, there was also ongoing communication in other ways between the school and the parents and carers whose children were participating in the programme, including informal conversations and comments at home via homework and reading records. The quality of dialogue between parents and carers and teachers improved, often to an extent that schools were surprised. The meetings revealed aspects about the pupils' development (physical, social, emotional) previously unknown to schools that has enabled them to adjust their provision accordingly. Parents and carers feel that they are listened to and schools cited examples of parents quickly responding to agreed targets.

Anecdotal evidence, reflected in the following comments made by parents and carers, indicates that initial parent and carer responses were very positive:

'Continuous targeting and reviewing pupil progress I feel is a fantastic approach as teachers and parents will constantly know next steps.'

'I have no idea what my child does every day as he does not have the confidence to discuss school issues and so I hope this Programme will help.'

'No-one has ever listened to me like this before.'

'Positive in the way that we know what his faults are.'

'Finding more activities to do together.'

'My child's behaviour has improved.'

Despite these very positive outcomes, some parents and carers did not feel that they fully understood the aims and intended outcomes of the programme. And one issue for some schools was how to succeed in getting 'hard-to-reach' parents and carers to come to the school for structured conversations. Despite these challenges, a number of schools produced carefully planned resource packs tailored to pupils' needs and targets. Parents and carers and pupils used these at home. They created a very good foundation for parents and pupils and carers and teachers to develop shared objectives. One school arranged themed weeks that were very helpful in equipping parents with strategies to support their children's learning.

Wales: Impact on wider outcomes (behaviour, attendance, well-being)

Evidence suggested that the programme had a positive impact on pupils' behaviour, well-being and attendance. In one example, where pupils were heavily involved in structured conversations there was a significant improvement in behaviour. The majority of schools felt that, overall, target group pupils demonstrated more positive attitudes to learning, including greater self-confidence, than before the programme began.

England: Overview of findings

The whole-school approach of Achievement for All has enabled school leaders to have a sharper focus on aspirations, access and achievement. The shift in teachers' attitude to teaching and their development of more inclusive practices through the Achievement for All framework – as a result of a greater focus on identification of those vulnerable to low performance – supports and encourages raised teacher aspirations and expectations for all children. Teacher development is reflected in the following comments made by teachers in schools working with Achievement for All:

- 'Our culture of engagement and aspiration has improved, and so lessons are more focused and behaviour is better, which also benefits other pupils.'

- 'Achievement for All has helped us focus on aspirational outcomes. Planning for SEND children is now more parent- and pupil-centred.'

- 'The whole school has benefitted from Achievement for All. We are seeing excellent progress in all children, along with more effective teaching and learning practices.'

Wales: Overview of findings

The findings from the Welsh Pathfinder programme are considered after the first year (three terms) of implementation and development of the programme. Overall findings show very positive early signs. Where the programme was well supported by school and local authority leaders, learners made good progress; this was beginning to be reflected in improved attendance, fewer incidents of poor behaviour and improvements in reading levels. This suggested that if it is appropriately supported by schools, local authorities and Regional Consortia, the scaling up of the programme could add significant value to the national priority of the Welsh government to reduce the impact of poverty on pupil achievement in the schools of Wales. Overall, the programme has been well received by the majority of Pathfinder schools. The use of structured conversations is widely regarded as a particular strength in developing effective communication with parents/carers. Evidence collected in some of the schools from parents, pupils and staff indicates very positive views about the effectiveness of the programme including increased confidence by parents in engaging with the schools.

Summary

Engaging in specific, country-focused activities has led to a richness of understanding enabling the Achievement for All programme to learn through research and evidence-informed practice. The following chapters develop the theme of leadership for inclusion through the 'Time to Lead' project developed in Lithuania. In so doing there is a particular emphasis on reviewing the role of the consultant. While consultant as a term has not been widely used in the delivery of Achievement for All, coaching is a key factor. The Lithuanian research project illuminates fundamental factors in understanding the relationship between leadership development and the model of practice adopted by consultants. There is also considerable focus on understanding the importance of the 3As principles – Aspiration, Access and Achievement.

PART THREE

Why School Leadership Needs to Change

CHAPTER SIX

The Lithuanian Context: Developing Leadership for SEND

School leadership is one of the main topics of European Union school modernization policy. Leadership development projects have been popular in the world for solving management problems. According to data provided by OECD, such projects are currently implemented in twenty-two countries. One of those projects, the Time for Leaders study, is important for policy makers and practitioners alike in terms of seeing how one country has approached changing policy that will impact on school leaders; their development and support and subsequent intended change in learning for students and pupils. To help understand the Time for Leaders project's intentions and the significant shifts in practice required, this chapter defines the school leadership landscape at the time of the start of the project. Funded through European Union Structural Fund, the project was first implemented in 2009. The chapter describes how an exploration of school leadership at the outset of the project, enabled a focused approach to developing an effective inclusive model/models for school leadership in Lithuania.

The context of Lithuania

Situated in the Baltic region, the population of Lithuania at the time of this research was 3,057,682 (as at November 2010). There are around 1,400 general education schools, 500,000 students and 45,000 teachers. Currently, the country is experiencing a demographic crisis because of emigration and reduction of birth rates. In the twenty years since gaining independence from the Soviet Union, the Lithuanian system of education has gone through major reforms in curriculum, testing of students' achievement and decentralization of governance. Education is presented by the government as one of the major priorities for the further development of the country; for example, 31 per cent of the EU structural support in 2007–13 was used for the development of education, innovation and knowledge economy.

Restoration of statehood in Lithuania in 1990 created new possibilities for social, cultural, economic and political development that corresponded with national aspirations. The historic shift in national development demanded a change in the attitude and perspective climate of the society: a basic comprehension of democratic values: a new political and economic literacy: and the maturation of a moral culture.

The government wanted to focus on special educational needs, bringing it more into line with the Universal Declaration of Human Rights, the United Nations Convention on the Rights of the Child and the Salamanca Agreement. The post-communist constitution (1992) was the first document to propose the integration of children with SEND into mainstream schools. Although children with SEND do attend mainstream schools and the number of special schools is decreasing, Lithuania still has a relatively high proportion of special schools, with a relatively high number of children identified as SEND (European Commission, 2013). In 2010/11 there were sixty-two special schools educating 3,860 pupils (9 per cent of pupils with SEND). In the same year, 41,600 pupils with special educational needs (representing 10 per cent of secondary school pupils) attended mainstream schools. Consultants, involved in the Nordic and Baltic project 'A School for All', are disseminating knowledge and understanding on inclusive schooling. At the same time, consultancy services, for schools and families, are provided through three national organizations: The Lithuanian Training Centre for the Blind and Visually Impaired, the Lithuanian Educational Centre for the Deaf and Hard of Hearing and the Lithuanian Centre for Pre-School Age Hearing Impaired Children.

These social changes will only be sustained if Lithuanian education is radically reformed and given new objectives. Between 1991 and 2007, the Seimas (Parliament of the Republic of Lithuania) passed several laws and reforms to enable the desired shifts in practice. These systematically addressed the structure of the Lithuanian educational system; quality and the creation of the necessary conditions for social-pedagogical self-development; and strengthening of relations between educational institutions of different levels – this included strategic analysis and monitoring and the role of the principal.

The State Educational Strategy for 2003–12 included a programme for special educational needs which set out the government's vision to

- implement the ideas of 'A School for All' into real Lithuanian school practice.

- ensure accessibility of all school types, introducing formal and non-formal educational programmes for people with SEN.

- provide an opportunity for people with SEN to learn in an environment that meets their needs and

- gradually decrease the number of special (boarding) schools and, along with this, to facilitate the creation of resource centres: the most advanced special (boarding) schools are to be transformed into resource centres.

(Source: European Agency, 2016)

In Lithuania, Education is organized through the Ministry of Education and Science (MoES) whose function is to formulate and execute the national policy. Up until 2010, the county governor's administration was implementing the national education policy at the county level, but since July 2010, this responsibility was passed on to the municipalities. Local municipalities are the founders of the schools and within their responsibilities there are some direct tasks related to school leaders, such as

- approving the description of functions performed by school directors (except for higher schools) and the list of the school's pedagogical staff.

- appointing and dismiss the director of the school.

- performing the evaluation of directors in state and municipality-maintained schools subject to the procedure established by the MoES.

- organizing in-service training for directors and teaching staff of schools (except for higher schools) and the process of their evaluation.

There are some features worth noting here in that there was recognition that while professional development was in place for school leaders, the legislation only recognized the director with no mention of shared, devolved, delegated or even system leadership. Secondly, it was only in the functional aspects of the role that directors were trained and that it was acknowledged that there needed to be a review of the preparation and support for school leaders, along with the need to develop leadership competencies (Snipiene and Alisauskas, 2010: 5–6).

The Project Feasibility Study (Adomavičius, 2010: 1), also focused on the acquisition of management competencies, highlighted the context of schools in the current climate:

In view of the optimisation of the school network in Lithuania, changing laws, urbanisation, and the overall situation in the country, the forecast is that the number of general education schools in Lithuania will decrease. The schools which guarantee a high quality of learning to its students are most likely to survive. In order to ensure a quality and comprehensive education, the management competences of teachers must be strengthened. If schools employ leaders, students will be taught in a more competent manner, they will be better prepared both psychologically and practically.

The Feasibility Study established that one of the biggest challenges was accountability: schools and teachers are evaluated not by the results of students' learning but by compliance to the standardized procedures. It was the right time to make changes and the *Time for Leaders* project was developed in this context.

The emergent landscape of school leadership roles in Lithuania

School leadership and leadership development had not been of paramount importance in Lithuania. The role of the director that has emerged in Lithuania was one where they are seen as overseeing functional tasks. The director was in charge of general education school: primary, basic, secondary, gymnasium or youth school. Directors are appointed by the founders of state and municipality schools for a period of five years according to the qualification requirements for the candidates approved by the MoES following an open competitive procedure. The Comenius report (Snipiene and Alisauskas, 2010: 4) outlined the key functions of the director's role as identified in the law of education passed by the Seimas in 2007; this includes the following five functions:

1   Directs the drafting of the school's strategic plan and annual action programme as well as the school education programmes, confirms them and directs their implementation;

2   Appoints and dismisses teachers, other persons involved in the education process and service personnel, also confirms their job descriptions in accordance with prescribed procedure;

3   Is responsible for making public the information for the democratic management of the school; ensures relations based on cooperation; the observance of the norms of teacher's ethics; transparency in decision making; the provision of information to community members; in-service for the teaching and non-teaching staff; a sound and safe environment that prevents any manifestation of violence or intimidation; as well as the formation of hazardous habits;

4 Analyses the status of resources allotted to school activity and management, initiates the implementation of the school's internal audit and is responsible for the results of the school's activity;

5 Performs the functions prescribed by the founder of the school and stipulated in the school by-laws and the job description.

To support the director, the leadership team also includes the deputy director for education and the deputy director for administration and economy. The deputy director for education has the responsibility for professional development within the school and also for the performance management of staff that can lead to pay rises. With the concerted effort of the central government to remove bureaucratic type jobs school leaders should be free to concentrate on implementing curriculum changes, with a critical focus on learning as they seek to integrate technological advances into the delivery of the curriculum.

It is apparent to all those involved in education at national, municipal and school level that the quality of leadership and management is critical to bringing about the changes required to implement the reform agenda in Lithuania. The issues relevant to school management fall into two categories. The formal targets for national development and, secondly, some of the contextual issues that affect the system as a whole. Together they constitute the education environment within which school directors operate and as such the issues that directors need to be equipped to address within a support and development programme.

In 2006, the Centre for Educational Leadership (University of Manchester) was approached by the British Council and the Lithuanian MoES to conduct a short scoping exercise into education leadership development in Lithuania. This study revealed that the quality of leadership is a prerequisite for introducing the changes required to put through the reform agenda. Subsequent to this, the National College of Teaching and Learning in England (International division) led on a leadership development programme, along with development of teacher competencies and advice on the process of appointing school directors.

The reform agenda raised challenges around the leadership and management of change and future working practices with government, school staff and the community. The context is within the imperatives of European wide, technological and societal change that need to be addressed as part of the development of Lithuania as a relatively newly formed European country.

In Lithuania 'the student basket' is an allocation of funding to schools for the purposes of student education. The amount is determined according to the numbers of students within the school. Any professional development for leaders would need to be funded by this source. Hence the necessity to engage all those involved within the system to ensure as many schools as possible buy into the concepts of the project to take the leadership of schools in Lithuania into a new future.

Shifting paradigms in the professional development of leaders

When the ministry developed the terms of reference and the components for the Time for Leaders project they wanted to make leadership development more systematic involving people from the universities to steer the programme development. Currently in Lithuania, there is no requirement for leaders to have a master's degree or any training in leadership. Therefore, the requirement by the ministry to start a postgraduate programme was to ensure it was leadership competencies that were developed.

The ministry having completed study visits to the National College for School Leadership in England and Leadership Centres in other countries were interested in developing a more work-based learning approach with experiential elements, action research and reflective practice components that were based on the needs of the school leaders rather than on what the universities could offer.

This more hands-on approach by the ministry is interesting as many elements had been decentralized, including initial teacher training, where the universities make the decisions regarding content and the regional centres in the municipalities and schools are left to focus on professional development with no national overview or programme. This shift in the role of the ministry is not to take back control but rather to reframe the activity and thus enable a more unified, systematic approach to leadership development across Lithuania.

Time for leaders: Taking it forward

Legislation 'governs' the management of schools in Lithuania, with the result that schools have little freedom to develop ideas and make changes. There was a general feeling at the outset of the project that school management needed to be liberalized and have financial independence; school monitoring should be aimed at results and not processes. The community should decide the aims of the school. Lithuanian education strategy did not at the time identify what it means to be a good school – everyone had their own ideas of what it might be like. During the scoping research the group felt it was important to be able to measure effectiveness. School management models could then be offered in the context of leadership.

At the time, government policy did not support the development of leadership in schools; there were different schools with the same system of management but the regulations did not allow schools to be unique. The general view was that schools should have more independence and this needed to be supported by school leaders. Every municipality is unique; this should be the same for schools with school structures enabling them to achieve results.

In considering the best model for leadership development, the following questions arose from the scoping activity and guided the initial approach of the project:

- What should leadership look like?
- What should the models include?
- Should they suggest one model or a variety of models?
- What model would be the best to encourage leadership?
- What would be the best management model?
- Should there be one head teacher for one school or one head teacher for several schools?

At the outset, the research group, in a unique position, explored the purpose of management and the purpose of schools. There was a focus on the mission and direction of Time for Leaders, with pedagogy at the centre. In light of the fact that greater independence brings greater responsibility, the role of the government was seen as that of having a series of expectations of schools as to what that responsibility might be; with the role of the municipalities and the schools being that of discovering how best to meet those expectations.

Educational, social and economic factors were considered and a shared notion of leading learning, leading people and leading organizations was developed. Evidence shows that the independence of schools enables them to identify their own values – the structure becomes the manifestation of those values and expectations.

Leadership was defined within an inclusive model piloted in England by Achievement for All (NCSL, 2009) where:

- Clarity of **vision** of leader is shared by the school or college
- **Commitment** to learning by the learner, teacher and community is evident throughout the school or college
- **Collaboration** (team work) between all members of the school or college community is demonstrable at all levels
- **Communication** is transparent, open and honest, reflecting the shared vision.
- **Leadership**, therefore, is owned by everybody; everyone is a leader.

Values of education and schools are important and require different models. Schools will develop their own aims and values and form a model according to these values. Schools might have aims but these are more effectively developed and realized when the government has a common view on education. Schools are for children, who are at the centre of educational endeavour; the outer circles are for teachers and community. Schools need to be orientated towards learning and other elements and should work back from what the child should be like when he/she leaves the school. The research group considered this within the context of a process not an end result, where there will be different schools with different ways or working. In ensuring that all schools place pupils and values at the centre of their plans, a strategic aim was needed.

Schools do identify values but they need to be identified and justified and put into practice. Leadership competencies, both hard and soft qualities, were identified and set. One of the competencies that has become more important is networking. The reality of Lithuania and other countries is that individuals have to grow up wanting to be a leader. At the time a lot of head teachers did not want the freedom, they felt more secure in obeying regulations. There needs to be a strong stimulus to make them change; in addition, there needs to be a focus on learning and finding a way of leading that will suit Lithuania.

Summary

This chapter has set the context for how the ministry of education in Lithuania approached policy change to the leadership of their schools. The aim of the Time for Leaders project and subsequent policy was to recapture the enthusiasm of teachers and school leaders that had been in evidence immediately after the country regained independence in 1990. The Time for Leaders project is a framework of practice intended to develop new models of schools and governance, leadership competencies and form a support infrastructure for educational leadership.

The findings of the Time for Leaders project will, through systemic change, empower the Lithuanian education community and every country across Europe to develop and improve schools; Lithuania, as the leading country across Europe on school leadership, should ensure there is a raised awareness across member states. The following chapter describes the detail of the project and its impact.

CHAPTER SEVEN

Time for Leaders Project

The Centre for School Improvement in Vilnius, Lithuania was successful in submitting plans to set up Time for Leaders using financial support from the European Union (EU) Structural Fund, an ambitious and highly integrated leadership project aimed at making a systematic impact on education in Lithuania. The intentions were to

- undertake a systematic approach to educational leadership.

- understand that educational leaders are reasoning and active creators of learning communities.

- promote sustainable educational leadership as the development of an in-depth universal learning.

- research the field of management and educational leadership in Lithuania.

- explore the 'state of the art' and ideas on educational Leadership.

- involve both educational and academic as well as business communities and experts from different fields and countries.

- stimulate discussions and public consultations with all stakeholders.

- motivate and inspire the education community.

Using the experience of the Centre for School Improvement, Lithuania, the project involved seventy-two Lithuanian and six foreign experts (at the forefront of educational leadership in their own countries) with a diversity of experience from educational establishments at all levels, organizational management, human resource (HR) management institutions, developers of training programmes, researchers, IT specialists, lawyers and economists.

Those involved in the project were placed in five areas (consulting, virtual environment, models of school governance, development of managerial competencies and a longitudinal study on the expression of leadership) and each area was further broken down into specific research groups, which have become the project teams. The first phase of the project began in September 2009 and was completed in May 2011. This chapter will consider the implementation, development and impact of the first phase of the Time for Leaders project.

The sources of data for the chapter have been taken from Lithuanian policy documents; conference activities with research teams; notes from meetings with individual research teams; reports following international visits; outcomes and outputs by research teams; interview notes from individual researchers; feedback from public consultations with the different interest groups; and case studies and stories of successful practices in leadership development.

Implementation

The theoretical framework, while centred on leadership, embraces policy change, transformation, schooling, leading learning, notions of performance, professional development programme design and models of support. There is a wealth of international research evidence that indicates that leaders make a difference and influence student achievement (Hattie, 2003; Leithwood and Levin, 2005). The modes of enquiry involved a team of international experts working with project teams consisting of university lecturers, head teachers, consultants, government officials and involved focus groups with practitioners.

The organization of the project teams was such that they all interlinked. Consultancy, school models and governance and managerial competencies are interwoven with support from the virtual environment. The intention from the beginning was to consider the model of schooling, how that linked shift in leadership approach and subsequent development of leaders within the schools. In addition, the project included longitudinal research on the expression of leadership. Each component was given a comprehensive brief with the required outcomes and outputs.

In practice, the work of project teams was very open and transparent: public consultations have been organized to present the direction of thinking of every working group, endorse the developments and elicit further ideas. The new ideas were tested with policy makers, teachers, teacher trainers and other interest groups in the process of their development. The open and public mode of project implementation helped to nurture support and encouragement of the educational community to the ideas of leadership development in the schools. Project teams were supported by a group of international experts whose mode of working is to facilitate sessions, question processes and practices rather than providing ready-made answers. This way of working has helped to ensure ownership of the project ideas and to sustain the enthusiasm and self-confidence of Lithuanian experts and participants in the project groups.

Leadership development within the project – underpinning theoretical perspectives

Across a number of European countries, teaching is becoming a master's-level profession. In developing the Time for Leaders project in Lithuania, it was important to have a strong focus at the outset on the key areas for each of the twelve research groups. The focus became clear through scoping and discussion, with the following areas providing the framework for research:

- Leadership learning in terms of content and focus – there is potential to integrate innovations in the field of curriculum, teaching and learning and the school environment.

- School effectiveness – based on the concept of leadership for learning.

- Power, people and politics – leadership changes at national, municipal and institutional level should support changes of teaching and learning and teacher's behaviour at the classroom.

- Systems leadership – expressed through moral purpose.

- Leadership – personal qualities such as collaboration, communication, listening, vision and commitment.

- Develop conceptual framework for the master's programme based on its purpose – to prepare high-qualification educational leaders, who are able to implement the leadership-for-learning mission at various types of educational institutions and organizations (i.e. to achieve multidimensional results of leadership in educational context: successful learning of pupils and communities).

Essentially, Time for Leaders is a project that engages communities of learners in considering the best practice underpinned by values. Fullan (2007) offers guidance in this area. This entails raising the bar and closing the gap of learning, along with treating people with respect and altering the environment for the better. In a similar way, Hopkins (2007) states that system leaders in particular measure success by raising the bar and narrowing the gap; are committed to improving teaching and learning; develop schools as learning communities; strive for equity and improvement; and realize that the classroom, school and system impact on one another and seek to engage with it in a meaningful way. Throughout the project, leaders at all levels were given the opportunity to contribute to the development of thinking and practice. Policy makers, school leaders and researchers worked alongside each other to understand how to improve the leadership of pupil learning in schools.

The project teams worked in the different areas of consulting, school leadership models, virtual environment, development of leadership competences and longitudinal research; each team used the same conceptual base, the concept of Leadership for Learning, established at the start of the project. Pupil learning is the pivotal point for leaders in education, followed by all other forms of learning (of teachers, managers, consultants, parents, etc.) aimed at providing a stronger background for pupil learning (Blandford, 2009; Knapp et al., 2006).

At the start and during the project the teams came together in a conference where members of the foreign expert team joined the Lithuanian research teams to explore each of the key areas. Subsequent conferences addressed specific theoretical perspectives to ensure all those involved in the project underpinned their work with the same conceptual base. Some of the perspectives that have been explored in relation to the work on developing leadership programmes and consultancy included: moral purpose; leadership learning; qualities of leaders; effective schools; power, people and politics; systems leadership; and theoretical frameworks. This section draws together what became the key issues for the teams that formed the approach to the project.

In addition to Leadership for Learning, another important concept for the project has been *Sustainable Leadership* (Fink and Hargreaves, 2006). Project leaders interpreted this term as the creation of powerful and equal conditions for learners, professionals, and the entire system in which leaders persistently and publicly focus their and the attention of others on teaching and learning by making learning the basis of their work.

A third strand of education leadership thinking to influence the project was System Leadership (Hargreaves, 2007). There are many meanings to System Leadership, each relevant for consideration by schools, municipalities and policy makers in Lithuania. System leadership can be played out through a school partnering another school (facing difficulties); leading a school in challenging circumstances; acting as a civic leader brokering networks/partnerships. When considering roles within system leadership, Hopkins (2007) offers those working as a change agent, for example, 'consultant leader'; someone who is involved in setting direction, developing people or developing the organization. Both system leadership and the roles within became increasingly important in influencing how the project wanted to approach leadership.

One further concept that was considered by the project teams was their 'level of influence' in terms of changing practice ultimately for pupils in the classroom. This arose during a project group meeting where discussion revolved around the theme of 'everyone in the educational system has a role to play'. However far removed from the classroom or learning base, leaders can influence how pupils and students are taught. How leaders behave and operate at school, municipal or national levels needs to focus on how they can contribute to better learning for all learners. A simple concept; but if teachers are, for example, shifting from a didactic model of teaching to independent learning where facilitated learning experiences are important, then they need to work with lecturers and consultants who operate in a more facilitative way to enable co-construction of knowledge. Those involved in designing and delivering the programmes also need to work in a different way. The project team applied distributed leadership throughout the system, so whether it is a politician in government or an independent consultant, a school leader or teacher, there is a responsibility to consider how to work with others and how to view learning and so on.

From the outset, there was a set of common objectives for each of the contributing teams to effectively address the central issue; this resonates with the theory on effective teams (Everard et al., 2004). The central team has ensured that the contributions of each member have been of the highest possible quality. This has enabled the project teams to improve their effectiveness and impact during the first phase of the project (Northouse, 2004).

Stage 1: The study of education consultancy services and supply of consultancy services in Lithuania and abroad

The first phase of the project was aimed at performing an analysis of education consulting activities and defining education consulting and consultancy services. In this stage the major focus was on the collection, systematization and partial summary of information from various resources.

Education consultants' activities are regulated by the Ministry of Education and Science of the Republic of Lithuania. The first phase involved a review of official reports of the institutions that have been training education consultants; interviews were used to verify the information. This was followed by a survey of education consultancy activities. This may be called an alternative to regulated consultancies. The survey was based on qualitative interviews with representatives of non-governmental organizations operating (or those that used to operate) in the field of education for the purpose of performing an analysis of the consultant's activity.

Provisions for education consultants' activities adopted by decree of the Minister of Education and Science of the Republic of Lithuania define a consultant (counsellor) as a person who evaluates school principals, deputy principals responsible for education, executives of the divisions that organize the education process, professionals who provide assistance to schools, pupils and teachers, and other members of school communities and consults them on the prioritized issues of national education policy, curriculum implementation, organization of the education process, school management and improvement, etc. The aim of education consultants' activities is to help school principals and teachers to ensure quality operation of schools and education. The Lithuanian Classification of Occupations states that an education consultant (counsellor) is an employee of the education system of Lithuania who explores and evaluates conditions of education.

Currently, 1,348 education consultants in forty-five areas of consulting hold a consultant's certificate. They received training at institutions licensed by the Minister of Education and Science of the Republic of Lithuania. In order to provide a summary of information, forty-five areas of consulting have been grouped according to trends of consulting: subject-specific consultations, management and improvement of schools, non-formal education of children, curriculum and implementation of the curriculum.

Many of the consultants (40.7 per cent) provide subject-specific consultations, with 36.4 per cent consulting on issues of school management and improvement, 12.4 per cent on curriculum issues and 9.6 per cent on curriculum implementation. There are 2,275 schools of general and non-formal education in Lithuania (1,364 schools of general education and 911 schools of non-formal education). On average, each school has just 0.59 per cent of the consultant's time, that is, half of their contracted time, equating to half a day a week per school.

In order to reveal the notion, emergence and development of the occupation of the consultants of general education schools, a qualitative research was initiated. Semi-structured interviews were conducted with representatives of non-governmental organizations operating in the field of education.

During the research, the types of consulting services were identified according to the following criteria: the suppliers of such services (informal and formal levels), target groups (individuals, small and large groups), and the content of services (standard activities in the schools, implementation of national strategy innovations). The interview aimed to clarify the origins of education consultancy activities in Lithuania. The starting point of such consultancy activities was considered to be the new qualitative seminars and training sessions of 1991–2 that aimed to instil a new approach to the education process.

During the interview two groups of consultants were identified, informal and formal (certified by the Ministry of Education) consultants. The following problems were identified in the training and activities of the formally operating consultants:

- Training of consultants was not based on quality criteria – selection was not clear, thorough assessment of the acquired skills and knowledge was absent.

- Knowledge multipliers were trained who frequently could not provide their opinion as they have not tested the experience themselves.

- Consultants were 'consulting' those who did not need consultations.

- Information provided by consultants was not adapted to a specific context.

- A general concept and system of how to further develop a consultant's activity was absent.

The respondents were asked to identify specific characteristics of the consulting services and how they differed from/were similar to other activities; they were also asked to define the competences of a good consultant.

The following problems for further development of consultancy services were identified by the respondents:

- sources of funding.

- lack of/unidentified demand.

- absence of a system/infrastructure for the supply of qualified consultancy services.

- Consultancy work is combined with consultant's other activities to avoid 'double' payment.

The premises for development of consultancy services included the need for consultations, an understanding of the benefits of such services, a different approach to problem solving, dissemination of information about consultancy services, the opportunity to request a good, professional consultant, and funding.

The study carried out in Lithuania (considered to be relevant to consulting issues) was based on four groups of initiators of consultancy services:

1 Consultancy may be initiated by the administration of various levels of education. Such consultations may include consultations related to various changes in the education system. For instance, the first systemic demand for consultants occurred once education streaming was introduced. Streaming in education called for consultants' assistance in implementing the streaming. Another surge in the need for consultancy appeared with the education system optimization and then at the start of the internal audit of schools. The administration of an education institution uses various qualification training providers to train consultants able to implement changes in the education system. The advantage of such initiatives is a clear and concrete demand on the part of the state, whereas threats are usually

related to the *en masse* nature of such initiatives and therefore poorer quality.

2 Education experts, scientists, representatives or the academic community may sometimes play a role in initiating a demand for consultancy. They may draw attention to innovations offered by education theories and changes taking place in the education communities of other countries and therefore recommend that the administration of education institutions pay attention to these changes. Some studies on the condition of education initiated by the Ministry of Education and Science show the type of consulting required in order that the Lithuanian education community would not fall behind academic innovations and European and global trends. These academic innovations may be implemented on a smaller scale by academic communities as well as organizations and consultants operating in a decentralized education consulting market. The advantage offered by consultations initiated by experts is the variety of consultancy services and one of the risks is that these innovations may never be approved.

3 The type and content of consulting may be determined by the needs of the teaching community. For instance, the study of the teachers' demand for qualification training may reveal different types of consultations, according to various parameters (time, duration, content, form, etc.), required by various members of the education community (teachers, managers, professionals of various disciplines, social educators, etc.). The advantage of consultations initiated on the basis of the needs of educators would be orientation to the needs of the various groups of the education community and one of the risks is to ignore educators' innovations that have not yet been approved.

4 Initiators of consultancy may be consultancy or qualification training providers operating in the decentralized education market. The advantage of such consultations is the wider variety of consultations and the disadvantage is primarily related to the fragmentary nature of such training, the price and an uncritical following of education fads.

During the course of the project it was relevant to compare consultancy activities in Lithuania with education consultancy models abroad with a more detailed presentation of the experience of two countries, Great Britain and Slovenia.

Education consultancy in England

The consultancy network in England is broad and a variety of consultancy practices exist at different levels of education. In broad terms it is about *process*, rather than *resource*, consultancy. The following four consulting models prevail: (1) public consulting, (2) specialist consulting, (3) empowering consulting, and (4) procedural consulting. Public consultations take place at all administrative levels – national, local and school level. The process is strictly regulated at national and local level, whereas no guideline regulation is applied at the school level. The specialist consulting model means that the consultant is solving a specific problem without affecting the institution itself or any individual internal processes. Specialist consulting takes place at all levels and usually repeats by including more participants. Such consulting is not regulated. Empowering consulting takes place only at local and school levels. According to this model, administrations of local education institutions are consulted by an inspecting institution, independent consultants or consulting institutions. The major part of consulting services in Great Britain is school oriented as the school is considered an institution that directly generates education results; the National College of Teaching and Leadership (NCTL) led the successful National and Local Leaders (NCL) initiative to drive school improvement through leadership development. All four models of consulting are represented at the school level. The model of procedural consulting is not prominent in the education sector. It is mostly practised for school managers' or young school professionals' training programmes developed by both public institutions and private consultancy companies. The manifestation of this model is most widely spread in psychology consulting of individuals.

Education consultancy in Slovenia

Slovenian consultancy practice is actively developing and has different levels. The following consulting models prevail: (1) public consulting, (2) specialist consulting, and (3) procedural consulting. Public consultations take place at all administrative levels – national, municipal and school – and the process is also regulated at these levels. The specialist consulting model is displayed when the consultant solves a specific problem without affecting the institution itself or any individual internal processes. Specialist consulting is used at national and individual levels. The model of procedural consulting is not prominent in the education sector. It is mostly practised at national level in order to prepare a school curriculum. As a result, study groups made up of teachers from different schools are established. These groups prepare the school curriculum and education consultants from the National Education Centre participate in the preparation process, summarize the various approaches, and make proposals to expert councils.

Impact

The first phase of this project brought many successful outcomes and outputs. These included: a competency framework for school leaders; outlines for formal and informal professional development programmes for school leaders; instruments for the longitudinal study; and a model of consultancy support and arrangements for networks, as follows:

Competency framework

During the initial stages of the project, it became more and more important to have clarity about the role of leadership in Lithuanian schools both as seen externally and internally. Establishing a clear competency-based framework for leaders and consultants led to the design of the required professional development programmes and the kind of support leaders might need. Tensions existed between current practice and intended practice, one where there was a relentless focus on learning; where leadership was devolved and so on to ensure all the underpinning theoretical perspectives were present. It was the responsibility of one of the project groups to research what this meant for various stakeholders prior to developing a framework for formal and informal professional development programmes. It was intended that the framework would underpin and inform the programmes.

Formal and informal programmes

Consideration was given to the key elements in both formal and informal programmes. Drawing on the findings of the feasibility study there was a recommendation to introduce a formal master's degree that would promote the managerial and leadership competencies of teachers. That recommendation was based on global trends; Lithuanian trends; genuine consumer need and identified current demand; and available opportunities for implementation of such master's degree studies. This endorsed the government desire from the beginning to include postgraduate study as part of the development programmes.

In addition, a study conducted in Lithuania indicated that teachers themselves felt that they lacked managerial competences in practice (Adomavicius et al., 2010). Furthermore, the feasibility study (Adomavicius et al., 2010: 7) concluded that,

> it will require a university which is experienced in both the field of education science and leadership. This experience must be proved by articles prepared at the university and published in the research/ professional publications, successfully implemented projects, and

participation of social partners in making and implementing study programmes. Therefore, both the lecturers working in the programme and the university that will implement the programme must have experience in providing training in management, education science and/or teacher training. At the project stage International School of Management (ISM) is involved in the development of the project. It was chosen because of the best (in Lithuania) expertise in leadership and management and it is being planned to involve other universities or educational experts to develop modules on education.

The ISM (University of Management and Economics established by BI Norwegian Business School) in Lithuania was involved from the outset of the Time for Leaders project; while they have extensive experience and excellent track record in business management they had not previously worked in the field of education.

Using current master's programmes as a stimulus, the teams considered the needs of such a programme to support/coach leaders and subsequently required teachers to

1   analyse the needs of the class/individual.

2   identify the strategies associated with each of the Aspiration, Access and Achievement (3As) strands (Blandford, 2008) which are needed to change the behaviours and actions of teachers in order to generate the desired outcomes and impact on learners.

3   determine the specific goal according to the changes needed; this may be a soft or hard strategy.

4   base the strategies and progress tracking on the 3As – Access (barriers), Aspirations (steps/skills) (motivation/mindset), Achievement (hard/soft strategies).

5   frame the 'story' with the 3As.

6   analyse each element of Aspiration, Access and Achievement.

7   determine the change in behaviour needed.

The development of the 3As model had been tested by the Teach First and Achievement for All programmes in England (Muijs et al., 2010; Blandford, 2011; Blandford and Knowles, 2013). From 2005 to 2010, Achievement for All and Teach First colleagues examined the impact of leadership practices on student learning. What emerged was a framework for focusing leaders' thinking and practice. Aspiration for learning refers to how students are motivated; their mindset – in essence the light bulb moment when they learn. This is developed by focusing on the desire and need to learn in the student and a desire to achieve at the highest level, in school, college/university and in the workplace. Access to learning focuses on removing the barriers to learning: physical, social, environmental, emotional, educational (and more). Once a student has the desire to learn, there is a need to identify what it is that prevents them from learning; leaders can then work with students, parents, teachers and support agencies to remove these barriers. Access can also focus on providing the student with access for future learning; as they transfer from class to class, year to year, school to school, school to college/university and, ultimately, into the workplace, leaders can ensure that there is access to future learning. Achievement is reaching the goal, set by the student's aspiration, provided by access to learning; this can be social, economic, environmental, technical, educational or political. Students can achieve through any number of activities, achievement being the fulfilment of the goal.

In the context of school leadership for learning, the importance of attainment in a formal educational sense cannot be ignored; thus examination outcomes were a goal. Achievement in schools is, in part, measured by student attainment; student aspirations and access informed and developed practice to meet the goals set within this context. The relevance of the 3As model to the Time for Leaders project is that it provides insight and relevance; leadership and learning in schools are inextricably linked to the development of the master's programme.

The development of a master's level route also relates to the Bologna Agreement (1999) that brought greater uniformity to the higher education systems in Europe and resulted in a number of changes within nation states. These developments presented a number of challenges in terms of access to literature in the Lithuanian language regarding innovative approaches to schools' leadership. The development group explored ways of capturing innovation within the system by using case studies. One further dilemma was where the accreditation would be located. In Lithuania the ministry issues a list of categories for the awarding of degrees and there is not a category for leadership. Discussions continue to be pursued with government ministers to resolve this issue and enable a programme essentially about leadership being classified within a management programme. As a consequence of this, the design and development of the informal programmes focused more on skill development of school leaders and consultants. The intention was that universities, municipalities and private providers would be involved in the delivery.

The master's degree studies needed to be beneficial both on the macro and micro levels, the aim being that more educated and trained teachers will effect better results of pupils and more efficient learning. This subsequently has a positive effect on the level of pupil education and general knowledge. The outcome might be that this would improve the quality of life and achievements of general education schools and the quality of the future lives and achievements of pupils.

Consultancy component

The consultancy component was directed towards the development of a model for consultative support for schools, as well as training programmes for consultants. The model of consultancy was based on the perception of leadership for learning. The ability to learn as a critical factor for all leaders in education: teachers, principals and consultants; Leaders are learning *practically, by and from practice* and consulting is considered to be the most practical learning. Mentoring and coaching provide exclusive conditions for the training of education leaders. Openness, self-confidence and dialogue are both premises and consequences of such training and expression. The first activity of the component was to examine the field and context of educational consultancy in Lithuania and internationally. The research data illustrated that there was a large workforce (around 2000) of so-called official educational consultants but that they did not consult; rather they transferred official government information or new trends of educational policies. That meant that in creating a system of consultancy to promote school improvement and leadership for learning, the negative image of consultancy had to be neutralized; the aim being to create a reliable system of selection, training, certification and recertification of consultants, as well as to develop an open information system on consultancy access.

Virtual environment (VE)

The VE working group started by defining an image of the education leader – a user of the virtual environment. There are many different environments and web pages for educators, so it is very important that leadership VE would not replace or copy existing tools but rather provide educational leaders with the services they do not receive elsewhere. The structure of VE was based on leadership roles and activities, such as consultancy, learning about leadership, 'bank' of new ideas and searching for support implementing them; this also included databases of documents and other tools necessary for everyday duties of educational leaders and sharing of experience and networking.

To strengthen leadership for learning, cultural changes are required in all levels of education. Attention should be paid to the following values essential for the implementation of the planned changes; respect (for an individual, profession, and agreements), trust, support and empowerment (responsibility and accountability).

Longitudinal research

The development of the methodology of the longitudinal study of changes in the expression of leadership was focused on the *study of trends in educational leadership* where the same instruments (indicators) were used at respective time intervals to study individual leaders (representative or target). The trend study was probably the most common longitudinal study and the group developed instruments for the regular measurement of the leadership expression and conditions at the levels of individual (student, parent, teacher and leader), school, school founder (municipality) and the state. The instruments of the longitudinal research were based on the understanding of leadership as a process alongside the position that a person may formally hold in an organization (Hogan and Curphy, 1999). The result of changes to leadership is high-quality learning and a strong relationship between leadership and the school or college as a learning organization, as Senge (2007: 44) stated:

> Leadership in a learning organisation becomes a mass phenomenon; the role of the leader is not uniform. Different people can be leaders in a learning organisation – this is determined by the nature of the problem, circumstances, personal competence, etc.

The leader in a learning organization influences others *not by his/her person* but by creating the *environment, situation or field*, which influences other members of the organization (Simonaitienė, Leonavičienė and Žvirdauskas, 2004). Systemic thinking provides a learning organization with the *conceptual basis* and provides the opportunity for the understanding of how people perceive themselves and the surrounding world, the *expanding of their field of vision, and training them to be open to ideas*. Identifying these areas has been critical as they need to underpin the content and processes of the formal and informal programmes so that leaders are prepared with the skills required for leadership of schools of the future.

At a national level there was the establishment of networks enabling sharing and partnership. Documentation of success stories agreeing on what a 'good' school, learning, teaching and management is. Changes in legal regulation: schools are given more autonomy; paid time is allocated for teacher initiative and cooperative networking. Local (municipal) level time is allocated for sharing learning through network meetings. Schools and individuals that share experience are valued. Schools and individuals that share ideas receive incentives and recognition. Municipalities provide schools with a platform to solve common problems and to develop a cooperative rather than competitive culture.

At a school level, formal and informal leaders were recognized and given the right to be active. Whereas highly qualified formal leaders were found to have time the time to work as mentors and consultants, informal leaders felt the support to move towards formal leadership. As a result, homegrown leaders appear. Schools have a real long-term strategy, school self-governance evolves and community initiatives are promoted. Finally, at the individual level it incorporated values, possessed and developed competencies, determination and motivation to take responsibility and action.

Separate research instruments were designed for each of the target groups, which ranged from teachers to professional support to pupils and students. Each questionnaire consisted of question blocks in different areas, such as successful learning, personal leadership orientations, attitude to leadership, creativity, self-assessment, reflection, work in school teams and participation in self-government.

Preliminary findings of the study showed that students and parents had the most positive attitude towards leadership development and expression closely followed by deputy principals. Teachers and municipality officers had much lower personal leadership orientation, as well as less trust to teamwork, reflection and participation in self-governance. Only 20 per cent of teachers wanted to take a leadership position in the future. Teachers had stronger belief about their individual influence to successful learning of students rather than institutional aspects of schools. Generally, the study showed significant differences in how different target groups understand and value a number of aspects of leadership; this suggested that there is a lot of potential in the development of leadership competencies of formal leaders, as well as teachers and other target groups. The findings of the longitudinal study will be used as the basis for the design in the leadership development programme.

The synergy between leadership, consultancy and school models

The Comenius report (Snipiene and Alisauskas, 2010: 18) usefully tracked the Lithuanian ministry's intentions for education. The process to shift education from where it was at the time of independence to where it wants to be in preparing twenty-first-century learners acknowledges the links between leadership development, consultancy and other forms of support for leaders and school models. As the project team stated:

> The main idea of the project is not just to train people, but to establish a safe risk environment for leaders to assume responsibility, use external help and become a support for others leaders. The main components of such incentives could be possibilities of studying leadership as well as leadership consultancy, virtual environment for leaders, publications, promotional career system, new models of school organisational structure, supportive supervision, etc.

From the outset of the Time for Leaders project, the areas of leadership (competency model), professional development and school models were closely interlinked. Each group was developed in conjunction with the others to create a way forward that ensured a consensus.

Continued challenges

After phase one of the Time for Leaders project, some significant issues that required further research and development were raised. The connection between leadership learning (content and processes) and the impact on student and pupil learning was considered paramount. Through the complexity, there is a potential to integrate innovations in the field of curriculum, teaching and learning and school environment but the challenge is that it needs to be addressed throughout the system and the project implementation adopted by the majority of Lithuanian schools. How school effectiveness is viewed needs to go beyond performance tables and an alternative view needs to be given to the notion of an 'effective school' which would be based on the twin concepts of leadership for learning and achievement for learning.

Changes at national, municipal and institutional level need to support changes of teaching and learning and teacher's behaviour in the classroom. The facilitators of learning on the formal and informal programmes need to be clear that how they work with participants is critical in shifting practices of learning for pupils and students. This all requires new models of professional development to embrace the cultural and role changes within the current and future leaders in schools and those that support them. This includes ministers passing legislation to recognize that the proposed programmes relate to leadership and therefore should not be classed as management programmes within the academic awards process.

The project has already been acknowledged as a having a critical and significant influence in shifting practice in Lithuanian schools (Snipiene and Alisauskas, 2010). The project leaders and international consultants knew from other projects. For example, 'Networks of Learning Schools' (2009–13) that only 27 per cent of schools in Lithuania participated in the School Improvement Project (2002–5) funded by the World Bank; this led to the desire to impact on a much higher proportion of schools if there is to be sustainable systemic change.

Final thoughts

The first stage of the project helped to create the conceptual bases for the implementation. At the next stage, the group strived to increase 'the critical mass' of leaders in education. The leader is any member of the educational community who is ready to take the initiative and responsibility for students' learning. Around 5,000 educators have been involved in different activities related to the project. In promoting the idea of 'leadership for learning' at all levels of education there needs to be a shared understanding that it is a united effort for the sake of students' learning. The intention is to develop and disseminate new forms of cooperation, public debate, consensus

building by regular leadership forums, public consultations and other forms
of networking.

Critical in moving forward with the Time for Leaders project is to
establish a new Lithuanian partnership model, involving state, business and
non-governmental sector through creating a School Aid Fund; Conceptual
models developed at the first stage were implemented at fifteen municipalities
and 50–100 schools.

These municipalities and schools were encouraged to develop unique
leadership development models directed towards the improvement of student
learning by efficiently using local potential and getting consultancy and
training support. Individual and organizational growth was documented in
written and audio-visual formats, especially individual experiences, success
stories and practices in order to give lively and inspiring examples for
other schools and educators. The research team also piloted selection and
training programmes for consultants, encouraging them to practise specific
consulting processes at pilot schools and municipalities. Approximately
300 leaders from national, regional and school level will be involved in the
master's programme and non-formal leadership studies and courses founded
on the leadership competencies.

In bringing the programme to this stage, many of the 'essential components'
of effective partnership (Zwozdiak-Myers et al., 2009) has enabled the Time
for Leaders project to develop and implement a more effective leadership
development programme. Although not all of the components contribute at
each level of change, a commitment to shared values and continual focus on
mission have strongly supported the achievement of the overall intentions of
the project. The contractual agreements between partners have set out clearly
defined roles and responsibilities. The open channels of communication,
culture of shared dialogue and flexibility has ensured that adaptation of or
change in role/responsibility necessitated by change at regional or school
level can be addressed quickly.

In addition, the Time for Leaders emphasis on innovation has resulted
in the implementation of a number of effective practices and processes
during the developments that have emerged from the teams. This can, in the
main, be attributed to the exemplary, sustainable models of partnership at
both organizational and people level and a continual drive for excellence.
This has underpinned the partnership since its inception and is reflected
in early findings. However, the particular focus within the partnership on
collaborative working, driven by excellence strongly contributed to the
development of more clearly defined roles and responsibilities.

Overall, the unique way of working in the delivery of Time for Leaders
helps to bridge the gap between research, theory and practice (Zwozdiak-
Myers et al., 2009). One of the strongest features of the partnership is the
emphasis on networking at all levels. This, however, is supported by strong
organizational structures, defined roles and responsibilities, commitment
to the purpose of Time for Leaders and a culture of open communication.

The Time for Leaders project is ambitious but the consolidation of the international team and support of the educational community will help to achieve significant changes in leadership development in Lithuania schools and begin to achieve the changes heralded at the time of independence.

Summary

This chapter has provided an insight into the importance of clarity in defining leadership. The emerging emphasis on partnership, networking and collaboration should not be ignored. Time for Leaders has provoked significant change in policy and practice in Lithuania applicable to other countries in Europe and beyond. The particular focus on understanding and implementation of the 3As model – Aspiration, Access and Achievement – is an indication of the strength of the Achievement for All framework. Equally, delivery through consultants (qualified, trained, monitored and evaluated) is endorsement of the Achievement for All delivery model.

The following chapters move to Norway and a change of focus, from leadership to teaching and learning. The implementation and impact of the Achievement for All framework, coaching model and evaluation methods are tested throughout the two-year engagement with the Oslo Municipal Department of Education (UDE) and its leadership.

PART FOUR

Why Improving Teaching and Learning Improves Outcomes

CHAPTER EIGHT

The Teaching and Learning for All Project: Norwegian Context and Case Study 1 – Lindeberg School

The Norway Schools Project started in June 2013, introducing a framework to improve teaching and learning based around the four Achievement for All elements, adapted for the Norwegian context:

- Element 1 – Leadership for inclusion
- Element 2 – Teaching and Learning
- Element 3 – Parent and Carer Engagement
- Element 4 – Wider Outcomes and Opportunities.

The Teaching and Learning for All project aimed to create an infrastructure and develop practices and procedures to promote improvements to the schools outcomes. Oslo Municipal Department of Education (UDE) commissioned Achievement for All to work with two schools in Oslo: the Lindeberg School and Høyenhall School. Both schools had previously adopted Tidlig Innsats Early Years (early efforts early years) (TIEY) and Fagtekst I Focus (subject text in focus) (FAIF) that aimed to address literacy and fundamental skills. TIEY is for Year 1–3 and FAIF for Year 4–7. TIEY is based on Australia's 'Early Years Literacy Program' – and has a fixed structure and organization with children working in 'stations' for a set period of time.

Both schools were underperforming against Oslo targets. An integral component of the programme is the existence of an Achievement for All coach, an experienced school leader with evidence of improving outcomes for children and young people identified with SEND. The coach in this project had sixteen years' secondary school leadership experience in a challenging London school. This chapter explores the context for the implementation and development of the Teaching and Learning for All project, and focuses on the first of two case studies in Lindeberg School describing how the Achievement for All framework and coaching methodology impacted on schools in challenging circumstances.

Setting the scene: The Norwegian education system

The Norwegian public education system is characterized by decentralization and autonomy. While education policy is developed and implemented by the Ministry of Education and Research, decisions for pre-primary, primary and lower secondary schools are made at the municipality level, of which there are 430 across the country. Decisions for upper secondary are made at the county level, of which there are nineteen. Schools and teachers have the freedom to select learning materials and decide on teaching approaches. Only 20 per cent of decisions are taken at the national level in comparison to an OECD average of 36 per cent (OECD, 2013). Although decentralization encourages and promotes local-level engagement and control, a clearly defined implementation strategy for education is lacking (OECD, 2011). This is one of the greatest challenges of the education system often leading to 'imbalanced governance and inefficient use of resources' at the local levels (OECD, 2011: 12).

Since 1997, children and young people spend ten years in compulsory education from 6 to 16 years (school years 1–10); following a national consultation this was increased in the same year from nine years. Transfer to lower secondary from the primary school is in Year 8, usually around thirteen years of age; all young people have the right to a further three years of schooling in upper secondary. With a relatively small population of five million people, almost one-fifth are under the age of fifteen (19 per cent; OECD, 2013).

Recent reforms have focused on raising standards in schools. The Knowledge Promotion Reform (2006), introducing a new curriculum, placed greater emphasis on pupil development of basic skills and knowledge through outcome-based learning. The action plan to raise performance in lower secondary education, based on the white paper – *Quality in Lower Secondary Education* (2011), focused on improving numeracy and literacy, along with classroom practices and school leadership, to promote this.

Although teachers enjoy a relatively small pupil to teacher ratio of 10:1 in primary and lower secondary schools, until recently there was little scope in school or local provision for professional development. This was addressed through the GNIST (Spark) initiative, a partnership between the Ministry of Education and the municipalities/counties (2009–14) aimed at increasing the quality and status of the teaching profession, teacher education and school leadership. Other recent initiatives have included providing better classroom support for students and enhancing the assessment system. School improvement and guidance for schools in challenging circumstances is supported by the Advisory Team Programme (2009).

A strategy for implementing the action plan for improving performance in lower secondary school (2012–17) was introduced by the Norwegian education authorities; the following four areas are guiding ongoing developments in education:

1 Define measure and communicate what good literacy, numeracy and classroom practices mean.

2 Identify effective practices for teachers, school leaders and municipalities to improve literacy and numeracy.

3 Develop support strategies for teachers to deliver improved outcomes in literacy and numeracy.

4 Strengthen school leadership to deliver improved outcomes in literacy and numeracy (define and communicate the role of instructional leaders; provide school leaders with training, support and capacity enhancement; and develop networks for school leaders to share and work together).

(Source: OECD, 2015)

Special education in Norway

Until the 1970s, special education in Norway was characterized by segregation, with a relatively high proportion of special schools. The turning point came in 1975 with the integration of the Special Schools Act and the general Education Act, which gave municipalities the responsibility for the education of all children, along with responsibility for SEN referrals, and promoted a more inclusive approach for children and young people with SEN. Although the two-tier system of special schools and mainstream public schools continued in Norway for a number of years, by the time of the Salamanca Agreement (UNESCO, 1994), the number of special schools had reduced; more children identified with SEN were being educated in mainstream schools.

The decentralized education system in Norway has resulted in a relatively good early childhood intervention service. For those identified with learning disabilities, priority access to pre-school education centres is given. Other innovative early intervention programmes include the Networking system, set up in 1999 in the Sorlandet Resource Centre. This enables children with speech and language difficulties to interact with a number of different people, thus supporting their early language development (European Commission, 2013).

The 1990s brought a number of reforms moving the special needs system closer to integration and inclusion in mainstream education. The Education Act promotes an educational system that is of 'equal quality and adapted to the circumstances and abilities of each child. This requires good learning environments, where the pupils experience an academic and social community which is pleasant and good for their development' (Norwegian Ministry of Education and Research, 2010/11: 5). All children in Norwegian schools receive an adapted education, that is, teaching adapted to individual needs. For those who need more support, they have the right to special education. The municipalities (for children up to the end of lower secondary education) and the counties (for young people in upper secondary and beyond) provide an Educational and Psychological Counselling Service (PPT) to support those experiencing developmental difficulties or having difficulties related to education (Utdanningsdirectratet, 2013). The service is provided directly to schools or health organizations. For schools, the PPT gives guidance on how to organize learning to better support pupils with SEN.

The reforms of the 1990s also saw the reorganization of special schools into a system of schools or centres for specific or more complex needs. The focus on inclusion in mainstream schools means that a number of special schools have or will become competence centres, where children with more complex or specific needs attend on a part-time basis. Statped – a national service, organized into four regions, with its base in Oslo – provides the support needed in local areas. Statped, currently undergoing reform, works across six core areas: acquired brain injury; complex learning disabilities; deaf-blindness/dual visual and hearing impairment; hearing impairment; speech and language impairment and visual impairment.

If a parent is concerned about their child's development they can request an expert assessment, with the referral coming through the school or health service. The first part of the referral is based on an examination of evidence (PPT speak to the parents and the school). This is followed by an expert assessment and recommendations and finally a follow-up. Recommendations usually lead to special educational support for pre-school children and special teaching arrangements for older children and young people. They are entitled to an Individual Education Plan, which includes the goals and contents of the special education; it is reviewed every six months. Although parents are now more involved in the expert assessment process and confirm their acceptance of the provision, collaborative working between parents and professionals is still an underdeveloped area in the Norwegian special education system.

It was within this broad focus of national change that Achievement for All was introduced in two Oslo schools. The following research is based on reports and interviews with the school leadership teams in Lindeberg School.

Lindeberg School context

Lindeberg School is an all-through school for children aged six to sixteen. It has approximately 400 students on roll. The school was redesigned and refurbished in 2009. The school has a large number of children from minority ethnic backgrounds. Dominant groups include Somali, Pakistani, Sri Lankan and North African pupils. The school is situated in a less affluent socio-economic area of Oslo. When compared to similar schools locally, it is underperforming in terms of attainment (Norwegian, maths). Improving reading is a focus for the school. Initiatives have been introduced to support attainment. Data has shown that this has had a positive impact as children progressed beyond the expected outcomes.

The Achievement for All coach visited the schools, in the main, once per month excluding August and December. The coach used a mixed paradigm to implement the programme. In the first year the coach delivered whole-school-level training, offering opportunity for reflection on current practice and activities to embed the theories and integrate into the school curriculum. The sessions with the leader group were more intensive and focused. Every visit was centred on presentation, discussion and sharing case studies relating to target groups. The sessions were designed to introduce the leader group and colleagues to the very latest academic research and good practice. The focus for each visit was decided by the head teacher in conjunction with the leader group and the coach. Hence, each visit was a combination of new developments and strategies with regular updates and monitoring. This approach continued in Year 2 of the project.

Lindeberg was consistent in the format used to present. Each session consisted of an update of the needs analysis developments, titled 'The Status Report' and was framed around the elements. This focused on progress data from grades 1–4, 5–7 and 8–10, and the evolving role of structured conversations. In a continuous enhanced focus on element 2 – teaching and learning, each visit also had a standing item of quality assurance and monitoring through observations and book scrutiny. An important feature would be a session of new learning as identified in the needs analysis or by the leader group.

Lindeberg objectives

The Achievement for All needs analysis pointed to several areas where Lindeberg School needed to improve. First, pupil results were not where the school wanted them to be. Results were well under the average of Oslo. As a first step the school wanted their results to match the Oslo average and to remain stable. Second, the school saw the need for even better cooperation with parents. The head teacher wanted the parents to be more engaged in their children's school work, to participate at parent meetings and to be more active. Third, the school wanted to raise pupil motivation and attendance. To achieve this, they considered actions involving groups of children and actions aimed at individual children.

Implementation

The head teacher took a whole-school approach from the outset, asking for staff to volunteer to do a needs analysis framed around the four elements. The questions/statements were translated to Norwegian by UDE to ensure that the teachers would not struggle with a language barrier. Teachers from all departments formed groups and they performed the needs analysis during the last two weeks of the school year. The results were summarized by the senior leadership team. The teachers stayed behind for a day after school closed for summer break and went through the analysis with the coaches.

Element 1: Leadership

Action 1 – coaching – new ideas and discussions

During the two years of the Teaching and Learning for All project the senior leadership team met with the coach on a regular basis. On our journey their knowledge has been important. Through every step we had useful discussions. When we, for example, decided that feedback and marking was our next step the coaches brought ideas from their schools. They also had a lecture for us on the importance of feedback and marking and theories on why feedback and marking is important. After our discussions we decided on what feedback and marking would look like at Lindeberg.

Action 2 – learning walks

One of the things the senior leadership team really appreciated were the learning walks we did with our coach. To be able to go into a class, make observations and discuss them with the coach was very useful. School leaders had all done learning walks and observations in the past, and we all had ideas about what to look for and how to discuss the lesson with the teacher afterwards. The teachers were, to varying degrees, used to leaders watching their lesson, but they all welcomed observations. We used the observation sheet based on our own standards for excellence in teaching (discussed in Teaching and Learning section). The head of the departments observed with the coach. Then we discussed what we had seen. After the discussions we agreed on how to give feedback to teachers.

Action 3 – working agreement – giving time

Heading into the two-year project period the senior leadership team knew that one of the main obstacles in school development programmes is the teachers claiming that it's too time-consuming. In our negotiations with the union we argued that we wanted to set aside time in the work agreement to be used on the different development projects. In autumn 2013, all teachers from the first to fourth grade were given at least two hours a week to follow up structured conversations with parents and carers. Because they were given the time in the work agreement it took away the excuses for having structured conversations.

Element 2: Teaching and learning

Action 1 – standards for excellence in teaching at Lindeberg School

We developed a standard for excellence in teaching during the autumn 2015. First we had a session with the teachers where they were told to look at John Hattie's research on what impacts pupils' learning the most. We wanted our work on the standards to be based on evidences and on teachers knowing their impact on children's learning.

Based on the first session and a short lecture on Hattie's research the teachers were divided in groups. Each group was told to come up with the five most important elements that should be in our standards. They were also asked: How do we meet each pupil's needs in order for them to have the best possible learning results? We went through the results of the group work with a group of teachers from all departments. The final result was presented to the teachers the following week. As shown in Figure 8.1 the standards are divided into three categories: academic content of the lesson, classroom management and teacher–pupil relations.

Each of the main areas is specified to more detailed standards. For example, by academic content we mean that the teacher

- is well prepared
- has 'get started' tasks that the pupils are asked to begin with when they enter the classroom – early start of lesson

- is engaging
- has clear lesson targets and the targets are known to the pupils
- uses a variety of methods/strategies/approaches to the topic
- differentiates instruction and adapts it to the pupils' abilities
- provides continuous constructive feedback.

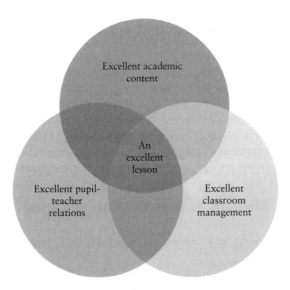

FIGURE 8.1 *Categories of the standard*

Each of the bullet points above were specified in a document with definitions. For example, by 'the teacher is well prepared' Lindeberg School means:

- I bring with me everything I need for class
- I've logged onto the computer before the lesson starts and have opened the programmes to be used
- all the equipment I will use during the lesson is prepared and ready
- I'm motivated for teaching when the day starts
- I'm punctual
- the lesson is well planned and structured.

The teachers are expected to follow the above standards when they teach at Lindeberg School. Based on the standard and the definitions we developed an observation sheet to use during classroom observations, which featured the points listed above.

Action 2 – tracking

To identify pupils struggling with academic performance we needed a better way of tracking academic progress. The school had in 2011 developed a plan for testing pupils at every level, and we had a lot of information about each child. But they lacked a system for tracking and using data to plan teaching. We started to use a tracking sheet developed by another school. The sheet was further developed to fit with our plan for testing. Together with the rest of the school, we introduced *gulltid*, an hour a week where teachers discuss pupils' academic progress and prepare action plans. The head of the different departments participates in the meetings on a weekly basis. The main focus of the action plans are the subjects Norwegian, especially reading comprehension and vocabulary, and mathematics, especially numeracy. Some also have action plans around behaviour.

In *gulltid* we identified the 20 per cent most vulnerable children in each age group, as determined by SEN and D or disadvantage. The first groups identified were in the first to fourth grade. The first selection was made around Christmas 2013 based on testing during the autumn. Each year group identified the pupils struggling and we had a discussion in *gulltid*. In some year groups we had more than 20 per cent of the pupils not reaching their targets, while in others most pupils were on track. After selecting the target group the parents were invited to their first structured conversation during the spring 2014. We also discussed the progress of the target group students regularly in *gulltid* following up on their progress. Different interventions were put in place. Some had courses intended to enhance vocabulary, some had reading recovery, some had lessons with a special needs teacher, but most of the work was done in a whole group environment. During the autumn of 2014, target groups were identified in fifth to seventh grade, and in early spring 2015 they were identified in the eighth to tenth grade.

Action 3 – feedback and marking

During spring 2014, we had a process where we developed a plan for written feedback and marking. We had a session where the teachers listed criteria on how the exercise book should appear. Based on those we developed an expectation for appearance of exercise books. The expectations were glued to the front page of the exercise book. We also developed expectations on frequency of written feedback. After quite a few discussions we decided on a feedback plan, which focused on encouragement and step-by-step instructions.

In the secondary phase, the teachers did not have a culture for giving feedback in exercise books at all. Before we started the process of developing a plan, the leader of the secondary had the teachers bring their exercise books and laid them on the floor. There was little evidence of teachers giving feedback. There was little evidence of formative assessment. The teachers also found the new routine too time-consuming. Even though the teachers objected to the changes, they started to give feedback. The first few months the main focus of feedback was on the appearance and based on the expectations glued to the first page in the book. During the school year 2014–15 the leadership team regularly asked the teachers to submit examples of feedback and we discussed the quality of the feedback with our coach. The comments were forwarded to the teachers.

Action 4 – differentiation

In autumn 2014 our coach had a whole staff lecture on differentiation. The teachers were challenged to do at least one differentiated lesson and invite the senior leaders to observe. Differentiation has been a focus of our learning walks this school year. We developed an observation sheet based on our standards for excellence in teaching. When giving feedback to the teachers they always had to reflect on their thoughts on differentiation in the lesson that we'd just observed. The aims of these conversations were to raise the teachers' awareness to differentiation. Some of our teaching methods like TIEY and FAIF are designed to promote differentiation. The pupils are divided into differentiated groups and all their tasks are supposed to be adjusted to their level.

Action 5 – expert teachers in Norwegian and mathematics

In autumn 2013, Lindeberg was granted funding from the state budget to hire expert teachers in Norwegian and mathematics. This allowed us to have additional teaching in both subjects. They are mainly used to differentiate teaching. They give the pupils struggling with mathematics and Norwegian extra attention and teach them in smaller groups. The expert teachers also coordinate subject plans, which contribute to the development of whole-school programmes. In addition, they are responsible for offering courses in accelerated Norwegian and mathematics.

Element 3: Parent and carer engagement

Action 1 – structured conversations

During the planning days in August 2013 we introduced structured conversations to all the teachers. They went through the basics of a structured conversation and also showed us some examples of conversations. In September 2013 our coach led a workshop with the first to fourth grade teachers. During the workshop they role-played different conversations practising asking questions. They were given a set of prompts/questions for each of the phases of a structured conversation that we had translated from English to Norwegian.

In November/December the target groups were identified and the teachers had their first structured conversations. Several of the teachers expressed that they were unsure of how to conduct the conversation, but they all tried. After all the teachers had had at least one structured conversation we had a session where they shared their experiences and gave advice to each other. They reported back that they had found the conversations useful. During the structured conversations they were asked to take notes and also plan next steps. In some cases, the teachers and parents agreed upon a new meeting, in other cases they followed up with frequent phone calls.

It is expected that teachers have a minimum of two structured conversations with parents of pupils in the target groups. These conversations are in addition to the regular teacher–parent conversations performed twice a year. The teacher takes notes from the conversations. These notes are filed in the pupils file. Structured conversations were implemented and developed across the school.

Action 2 – parent meetings

Attendance at parent meetings has been on our agenda since day one of our involvement in the project. At a seminar in April 2014 we had a workshop with the teachers. The workshop resulted in ideas for topics on parent meetings. The SEND coordinator and the parent counsel also had ideas for parent meetings.

Some of the ideas that we've used in school this year are: pupils showing parents the work they've done at school, group work, different topics (e.g. bullying), bilingual teachers attending the meetings, parent meetings for the major language groups (Urdu, Turkish, Arabic). For instance, at the seventh grade parent meeting in September 2014 the pupils contributed with performing songs, reading poems and other things they had prepared in advance. Parents wanted to see their own child performing and therefore participated in the meeting. Traditionally we have given the parents a lot of information at the meeting. This year the parents were divided into random groups and had a discussion around the topic of expectations. What do they expect from the school and what do they expect from each other? Prior to the parent meetings the teachers send a written invitation and the parents are expected to reply if they're attending or not. The teachers also send text messages to remind the parents the day before the meeting, and sometimes also the same day. If parents do not reply the teachers are asked to call them the day before the meeting.

Action 3 – positive text messages to parents

We want the teachers to send at least three positive text messages about pupils to their parents every day. Within a short period, every child should get a text message sent to their parents. The idea behind this is that if most of the communication with the parents is positive, it is also easier to talk about the negative. And all parents want to hear from others that their child is doing something nice.

Action 4 – homework plan

In spring 2014 we developed our homework plan. We wanted the plan to look the same in every grade. We decided on a layout that was to be used. Now parents having children in different levels see that the homework plan looks the same throughout the school, whereby the details and time are set for each half-term.

Element 4: Wider outcomes

Action 1 – inclusion manager

In January 2014 we hired an inclusion manager. We had seen the need for someone to help us with vulnerable and challenging children at Lindeberg School, especially in secondary school. The inclusion manager is a former police officer. Some of the inclusion manager's tasks are:

- Follow up on pupils not coming to school
- Be visible in the school environment
- Talk to and follow up on vulnerable children – difficulties at home, problems with interacting with other pupils, behavioural issues.

Together with the SEND coordinator he is responsible for developing action plans for pupils with different challenges when it comes to behaviour and school refusal. Our inclusion manager also collaborates with the field team, the district administration, the child welfare system and the police.

Action 2 – Tidlig oppstart (Early start)

Tidlig oppstart began after winter break. We had seen a tendency that pupils were going to class late. Our inclusion manager (*miljøterapeut*), the SEND coordinator and deputy head worked out a plan for *tidlig oppstart*. They informed all the pupils about the new routine and a letter was sent to the parents. All pupils are expected to be on time with all their books and equipment ready. As soon as the teacher closes the door and starts taking attendance the lesson has started. Anyone coming after that is noted as late. On Tuesday and Friday mornings all the pupils who had arrived late are asked to arrive between 7.30 and 8.15 for an early start. The parents get a text message notifying them about *tidlig oppstart*. If the children don't show up on time, their parents are called by one of the senior leadership team and they get a second chance the following Tuesday/Friday. If they have more than one no-show our inclusion manager calls the parents to follow up on the child's absence and make action plans.

Action 3 – management of student absence

During spring 2014 the SEND coordinator developed a plan regarding prolonged pupil absence. In detail the plan states what's to be done and who is responsible. The first day of absence parents should notify the teacher about the reasons for absence before noon. If they don't notify the teacher, the teacher phones them. If the pupil is still absent after three days, the teacher should contact the parents to further investigate reasons for absence. On the fifth day of absence, the teacher notifies the SEND coordinator and senior manager. After eight days of absence, the parents are summoned to a meeting. The aim of the meeting is to develop an action plan to get the child back to school.

Action 4 – homework support

We offered homework support to tenth grade pupils struggling with mathematics. They were selected on the basis of their poor results in mathematics and were supported by our maths coordinator. At winter break, tenth grade pupils were invited to participate in winter-break-school in mathematics. The focus of the lessons was the upcoming exams and how to succeed. On Saturdays, tenth grade pupils could sign up for maths lessons. The school also cooperated with Save the Children programme. They offer homework support for pupils in the fifth to seventh grade. About twenty of our children participated in the programme.

Action 5 – rewards

In January 2015, the student council came up with the idea of giving out rewards to pupils. They decided on five different categories:

- the compassionate classmate – shows respect for others, helps fellow classmates if they're bullied, does not swear, do not discriminate, does not bully, includes classmates
- the most enthusiastic and dedicated pupil

- attendance – shows up on time and attends class
- the academic climber – the pupil that improved most
- best academic results.

The awards were handed out at an assembly the last day before winter break. All the pupils in secondary were present, and the head of the student council announced the winners of each category. Copies of all the diplomas were hung on a wall of fame outside the classrooms of eighth to tenth grade. The pupils receiving an award also got a gift certificate to go to the movies. We had another award ceremony the day before Easter and are planning to have a third ceremony the last day of the school year (see Figure 8.2).

Other actions initiated by Lindeberg School to enhance pupil well-being include lunch break activities, breakfast, pupil-run canteen, student survey on bullying and collaborations with other organizations to provide play and recreation activities. During the Nobel peace prize arrangement in December 2014, pupils from seventh grade participated in arranging the Children's Peace Price Concert at Rådhusplassen. They interviewed the peace prize winner Malala Yousafzai on the stage in front of more than a thousand children and broadcasted the interview on national TV. During the Teaching and Learning for All project, three of our pupils in secondary participated when Save the Children wanted to make a report about being a child in a poor family. The report gives advice to politicians. In June 2015 the report was launched at Lindeberg School. The Minister of Children, Equality and Social inclusion was invited and answered questions from a youth panel.

FIGURE 8.2 *Copies of diplomas on a wall of fame outside the classrooms*

Impact

The following section provides a description of the impact of the Teaching and Learning for All project on systems and practice within the school. The impact on teaching and learning is demonstrable in qualitative terms. Quantitative outcomes are also evident, particularly in attendance, reading and maths, whereby pupils met or exceeded expected outcomes.

Element 1: Leadership

As a result of using the Achievement for All framework, Lindeberg School has strengthened its leadership: which is now dynamic, courageous, risk-taking, reflective and strategic. They now have high expectations of staff and students alike. There is a changed culture towards more openness and professional trust. This can be seen through a number of new structures and measures:

1   The leader group is **strategic**. They are now guided by evidence and the needs analysis rather than just custom and practice. By scrutinizing the assessment data, the team has identified which groups of students and parents need intervention. The data clearly showed a marked underachievement in maths (also an Oslo target) and Norwegian. Hence, Norwegian and maths have been the focus for much intervention, improving Norwegian across the school by 33 per cent and maths by 20 per cent. The leader group continues to track and monitor closely, not just collecting data but using it to inform practice. The establishment of baselines has enabled the tracking of progress as well as attainment. Another example of being strategic and evidence driven is the use of the Elevundersøkelsen. This evidenced improvements from 2013 to 2014 in areas such as parental engagement, feedback and marking, safeguarding and the environment. The leader group has exploited the results of this project to further drive its next steps.

2   The leader group has established practices to ensure **accountability** and **quality assurance**. Standard operating procedures and protocols to embed key developments such as marking have led to a marked improvement in the standard of feedback in the books. Staff have been receptive to training and monitoring. They have engaged and some actively encouraged and welcomed this level of scrutiny.

3   The leader group has **distributed leadership** to sustain and embed developments; to empower and add capacity and to

ensure consistency. The following are examples of this **devolved leadership**:

- teachers as leaders in the classroom
- leaders of the grades/phases
- leaders of the subject
- the use of *Gulltid* to evolve and monitor developments in the grades – this is weekly
- the creation of new posts. An exciting example of this has been the employment of Christian Hinch as the inclusion manager.

4   The Achievement for All framework has afforded the leader group the opportunity to **manage significant change** with the partnership of the staff. They have

- shared changes with whole staff through the mandate of the needs analysis.
- sought whole staff input on key policies and procedures such as 'the good lesson' and the feedback policy.
- created and formalized dedicated extra **time.**
- given small but significant gifts for those undertaking work associated with the changes.

Element 2: Good teaching and learning

An important impact of the programme has been a further shift in culture from blaming external factors and abdicating responsibility towards acknowledging the powerful role of schools in arresting underperformance. By accepting the Achievement for All programme and all of its strategies, there is an acceptance, albeit, tacitly, that schools can and do make a difference. The introduction of and engagement with the Achievement for All framework over the past two years is testimony to the teaching staff's acceptance that standards needed to be raised. Staff were keen to be observed, quality assured and held to account. They have and are accepting culpability. The following describes the impact of the Achievement for All programme on changing practice.

Teaching and learning: Use of data tracking and monitoring

As a result of the Achievement for All framework, Lindeberg is using data to drive interventions. The school was quite used to central collection of the results of summative assessments/tests. However, they were data-rich but information poor. The information did not guide whole-school strategies and policy closely. Nor did it inform planning for lessons. The following examples illustrate the monumental shift in paradigm. This forensic analysis and targeted intervention with specialist staff has brought about accelerated progress for the targeted cohort. We see evidence of the closing of the gap.

Data analysis and tracking
As a result of the Achievement for All programme and the intensive training around provision mapping, Lindeberg instituted a formalized tracking system and 'testing plan'. They actively turned data into **information** to guide their teaching and interventions. Through the *Gulltid*, they identified underachievement and low attainment and met weekly to forensically analyse and monitor, track and discuss progress interventions and importantly their impact. All but one of the students in the project have been lifted out of level 1, the lowest level of attainment. This system has now been extended to include behaviour.

Interventions and provision mapping
In grades 4, 5 and 6, the leader worked with their teams to create provision maps. They used the same format for each group:

- analysis, to guide the
- interventions,
- led by the SEND teacher
- guided by the skills required by the public test.

In grades 4 through 6, there has been a big push on literacy. The leader coached and led phase teams in analysing patterns of low attainment and the returned analysis from the national rests. The resulting intervention has been to group the students accordingly into small groups with the SEND teacher. They carried out intensive acquisition and drilling of new vocabulary and concepts as well as reading and writing skills. This drilling through test papers and focusing on weaker skills has also been used to prepare students for the Oslo digital test (literacy) taken in grade 6.

Lindeberg has also used the data to identify students in need of enhanced and intensive numeracy intervention. Mathematics results throughout Oslo are lower than expected. This is also the case at Lindeberg. The school deployed a range of strategies to upskill the students. Tight analysis of the exam results by question gave the team information regarding the numeracy skills they needed to target. They 'drilled' the students and retaught topics to 'fill the gap'. The 2014/15 data shows the AfA cohort making accelerated progress beyond expected levels.

Teaching and learning: Raising standards in the classroom

Lindeberg has taken a laser light focus on pedagogy. This is where most of the developments have occurred. The Achievement for All coach worked closely with the leader group to develop strategies to lift standards in the classroom: clear characteristics of excellent teaching with mechanisms to know the situation and to further drive up standards.

Developing the lesson standards – 'standards for Excellence'
This followed the discussion about what constitutes a good lesson. The leader group led a series of meetings with the staff and phase representatives. These meetings encouraged the staff to discuss academic thought and consider evidence. The result was a comprehensive list of standards under the three main headings: (1) excellent academic content, (2) excellent pupil–teacher relations and (3) excellent classroom management. As these standards were developed in partnership, there is an expectation that teachers follow them. This was new and constituted a cultural shift towards consistent practice and alignment.

Quality assurance and monitoring: Observations and learning walks
The coaches ran a series of sessions on how to observe and how to give quality feedback to the staff by using a coaching model. This drew on the good practice from the English Ofsted guidance and the training materials from the Association of School and College Leaders (ASCL), the head teachers union in the United Kingdom. As a result, Lindeberg developed its own observation sheet. It captured the key areas of the lesson standards. This gave the leader group the mechanism to know and evaluate standards in the classroom.

The team also carried out themed learning walks to monitor the embedding of differentiation. These furthered the close governance the leadership now had over the quality of teaching and learning. As the standards were devised in partnership there was a higher level of 'buy-in' and transparency and a desire to improve. The visits to the lessons were a combination of announced and unannounced.

As a result of the programme, Lindeberg uses a range of quality assurance strategies: learning walks and lesson observations. Staff have an open door policy and welcome the level of scrutiny. There has been a raised expectation of teachers: the quality of planning and delivery and an increasing appreciation of the importance of regular feedback. The students, as a result, are more motivated and take pride in making great effort. This is discussed under the next section.

Assessment: Marking and feedback, book scrutinies
The Achievement for All coaches ran workshops with the leader group exploring **why** and **how** to assess student work. The coach brought examples

of good practice from primary and secondary schools. The leader group led a series of staff meetings to establish and echo the coach meetings: the social and academic importance of formative feedback, high expectations around presentation, frequency and quality comments to ensure student progress. The school developed clear standards for marking and feedback.

The existence of the plan, marking standards and book scrutinies has been impressive. There has been a significant change in teachers' attitudes to marking and feedback. There is more regular feedback, comments on the presentation and an increasing link to the objectives (knowledge and understanding). Students are taking more pride in their work. They are given time to reflect on the teacher comments and make the necessary improvements.

Differentiation

The Lindeberg leader group made differentiation a key focus of the raising of lesson standards. They carried out themed learning walks against a specifically devised observation sheet. Teachers had to show planning and the leader expected reflection on differentiation in the feedback after the lesson.

Differentiation is now an expectation. It is a key component of a 'good' lesson. There is a realization that every student has an entitlement to make continual progress. Teacher barriers to differentiation are being overcome with a solution-focused approach and a growth mindset. Lack of time is being resolved through the leader group building planning time into the teachers' hours. This has been negotiated with the unions and is illustrative of the 'collective bargaining' approach that the head teacher and the leader group have adopted over key strategies. Also, staff have been encouraged to work in a collaborative way and use joint planning. Joint planning, along with the promotion of external short courses, has also gone some way in meeting the challenge of the perceived lack of expertise around differentiation. Teachers report that they are keen to grow these skills.

In the lower school teachers have embraced differentiation through the use of stations. Teachers throughout the school have started to use the Bloom's Taxonomy. The coach encouraged the teachers to display the taxonomy in their department areas to aid their planning. There has been a growing understanding of the hierarchy/ladder of progression within the subjects. This will have to be deepened to attain the graduated approach needed for effective questioning, feedback and devising differentiated work.

The developments in differentiation have been further embedded by the appointment of expert teachers in Norwegian and mathematics. They have been central to planning, differentiating and identifying and teaching smaller targeted groups. This paradigm of 'plan, do and review' with the use of prior attainment data, has also been used in the upper school to target the more able students. Lindeberg's expert teachers now offer these students accelerated Maths and Norwegian. These teachers have extended this programme to the students of the local school, Jericho. Such is the growing confidence and mindfulness that Lindeberg is now performing the role of a lead school with their neighbouring school.

Motivating students
The Achievement for All coach facilitated a leadership session on how to motivate students. Discussion considered the theory of intrinsic and extrinsic motivation. Intrinsic being more rewarding and lasting. The role of teaching and learning was also discussed. Teacher enthusiasm, curriculum relevance and accessibility were identified as key notions to be worked on. Student motivation underpins all of the other strategies. Challenging and engaging lessons, work that is assessed with feedback to further motivate and a meaningful reward system would go some way to motivate and engage the students and thus accelerate their progress.

Element 3: Parent and carer engagement

Lindeberg has deployed a range of strategies to engage parents in their children's learning. These include:

Structured conversation

As a result of the introduction of the structured conversations, staff are developing active listening, coaching and target-setting skills. Staff have co-coached each other to strengthen their skills. The relationship with the parents is increasingly one of partnership. Hitherto, 'hard to reach parents' feel more respected. They are listened to and are more empowered to support the child at home. The parents feel that they will be able to contact the school, if needed. This is an important cultural shift. Staff also have the mandate to hold parents to account through the target setting. Parents are in a 'contract'.

To date, grades 1 to 4 teachers are using the structured conversation model to supplement the traditional meetings with parents. Grades 5 to 7 have started using the framework and from September 2015, this will roll out to grades 8 to 10. Attendance at meetings in general has increased from just over 50 per cent to 95 per cent. Also, the nature of the engagement is more proactive and there is a closer link to academic progress rather than behaviour concerns. This is impressive. The structured conversation is now an important part of the student's provision map.

Themed evenings: Anti-bullying and safe digital use

Efforts are made to engage reluctant parents, making sure that communication is comprehensive: staff text, email and phone home. In addition, the school targets parents of vulnerable students. The evening's atmosphere is relaxed and relations are forged in a non-threatening way.

This draws on the latest research and the very best practices. It also illustrates the school's willingness to boldly take risks and break down barriers.

Engaging the parents has become more strategic and proactive. There is now a changing mindset. Parents are not seen as unquestioning and difficult but key stakeholders in an evolving partnership. By courting more positive communication there is a growing trust between the school and the parents. School is not to be feared or left alone. The Elevundersøkelsen (student survey) 2014 records an improvement in how parent engagement is perceived by the students.

Element 4: Wider outcomes

As a result of the Achievement for All framework, Lindeberg has developed a range of strategies to create a stronger and more positive ethos for learning. They have also been inspired by their visit to Hampstead School, Camden, England, where wider outcomes are considered central to there is a child's success. To this end, they have introduced strategies to improve attendance and punctuality; they are promoting and rewarding positive behaviours for learning and strengthening systems to safeguard students' emotional health and well-being. Much of this has been achieved through the creation of new middle leader posts. These posts add capacity while drawing on the skill of those who have very specific expertise. This heightened awareness has also resulted in the leader group leading and coordinating new procedures and practices to augment the developments as indicated below.

Attendance

Great efforts have been made to reduce the levels of non-attendance, particularly school refusers. This is largely due to a school-based system coordinated by the SEND coordinator. There are set actions depending on how long the student has been absent. The system is clear, non-negotiable, yet empathic and supportive. Teachers are pivotal to the system, if low level. When the non-attendance is more serious, the case is escalated to more senior, specialist staff. This may include a meeting between a leader and the family and a support plan with targets. In 2014, attendance increased from 85 per cent to 95.4 per cent and now is more in line with the Oslo figure of 95.5 per cent. Long-term school refusal has now dropped to one student from five in the previous year.

Creating a positive learning ethos

Inclusion manager
Lindeberg appointed an inclusion manager to coordinate interventions for those students underachieving due to problems at home and/or poor

behaviour. This role also has added capacity. The leader group is freed up from the time-consuming cases of a small group of students. This role continues to evolve. To date, it is impactful and value for money.

Analysis showed that the students' strongest misdemeanours were around lateness to lessons, leaving lessons without permission and arriving late to school. To remedy this, the school has introduced early morning sessions starting at 7.30. This has led to improvements in punctuality. Lateness to school and lessons and instances of leaving lessons have reduced. Students are increasingly in the right places at the right time. Importantly, the learning process of the concerned child and others in the lesson can start more promptly. Students, hitherto, disinterested and apathetic are running to lessons. Records and tracking has shown that less students are being put in the *Tidlig oppstart* and the group of regulars is decreasing.

Rewards and/sanctions

As dictated by good practice, the most effective way to promote good behaviours is to actively, regularly reward students displaying positive behaviours. To this end, Lindeberg has introduced a new rewards system celebrating a positive ethos under the following categories:

- the compassionate classmate
- the most enthusiastic and dedicated pupil
- the best attendance and punctuality
- the most improved – effort
- the best academic results – achievement

These were awarded in an end-of-term assembly (February 2015) and copies of the certificates were displayed on 'the Wall of Fame'. Students displayed enthusiasm, respect and support. This is certainly indicative of the holistic cultural shift.

Safeguarding

A safe place to be

These last two years have seen the development of a series of activities to keep students on site and safe. There are supervised activities at lunch and breakfast (on pause for now) and canteen provision. The school has continued to fund the free fruit initiative. These initiatives are testimony to the enhanced awareness of the emotional and social needs of the more vulnerable. The school continues to sponsor the training of peer counsellors who are central to the school's anti-bullying strategy. They visited Hampstead School in 2014.

The school provided special maths homework support to the tenth grade, who are preparing for examinations. The school also seized the opportunity to cooperate with the charity Save the Children to procure more homework support. This is amid a school culture that traditionally has left after-school activity to youth services. The student survey (Elevundersøkelsen) for 2014 recorded improvements in perceptions of feeling safe. These results further inform developments.

Extracurricular

As a result of the Achievement for All framework, Lindeberg has taken advantage of external programmes for the more vulnerable students. They have understood the need to provide the opportunities that will increase the students' cultural capital. It is known that vulnerable students rarely take up extracurricular and they certainly do not do many activities out of school. To this end, Lindeberg has procured partnerships with **Tveten Gard** for students at risk of dropping out of school and opened up the premises for **Omradeloft Lindeberg**, a community-based organization to promote community activity. This also serves to raise the profile of the school in the area and increases parent activity in the school.

Conclusions

Lindeberg's adoption of the Achievement for All framework has been transformative. The school has established new systems and procedures to support raising standards; there is a changed culture around wanting to improve teaching. Staff are keen to learn and develop. There is a growth mindset. The leader group has fostered 'reflexive' practice. Such reflection and the desire to improve outcomes for the students and to strengthen teacher skills have meant the engagement with the latest academic research, training and best practice. Solutions to underachievement now lie not in the home or in the community but in the school, particularly the classroom.

As the Principal stated:

We've taken a lot of actions over the two years of the Teaching and Learning for All project at Lindeberg School. We still need to make these initiatives a part of the culture of Lindeberg School, 'This is how we do things at our school'. There is a need for further development from structural thinking to quality.

The following chapter moves to a neighbouring Oslo school facing similar issues with additional leadership challenges.

CHAPTER NINE

Teaching and Learning for All Project: Case Study 2 Høyenhall School and Project Recommendations

This chapter follows on from the previous chapter, in that it explores the implementation and development of the Teaching and Learning for All project in Høyenhall School in Oslo. Like the previous chapter, it is presented as a qualitative case study spoken in the words of the head teacher.

Challenging our practice has helped us to reflect, plan and improve.
(School Principal – Oslo)

Høyenhall School context

Høyenhall, a mainstream school in the East of Oslo, has approximately 600 students on roll. In 2013 the school was underperforming against other schools in the area. It caters for increasingly diverse communities, some children from more economically stable backgrounds and some from more recently arrived and ethnically diverse communities. Høyenhall has recently gone through some turbulence in senior leadership with 3 changes of head teachers over a short period of time, and changes to inspectors and deputies over the two-year period of the Achievement for All programme; this is widely recognized as having impacted negatively on school development. Since September 2014, there has been more stability and cohesion to the team, which has manifested positively on school improvement.

Element 1: Leadership

Milestone 1: When management has a common understanding of the project and is accountable for its implementation

When the school started the Teaching and Learning for All project, the head teacher had been employed at the school just less than six months. When the school year 2013/14 started, a new inspector was hired as well. She later became assistant head teacher. With such a new leader group, there was a need to determine a common understanding of the project and to create a positive cooperative structure in the leader group. The staff stated that they wanted more immediate feedback and clarification from the school leaders, and thus a more efficient leadership. The structure of the leader meetings was established. Each week a meeting is held, with a topic related to educational development and Teaching and Learning for All as well as one administrative leader meeting per week, with topics that include operations, general information and sick leave follow-up. This has helped us become a more structured leadership, working more systematically with educational development while simultaneously becoming more efficient because we can make decisions more promptly in a hectic work environment. Another area of improvement is to set aside more time to follow up pupil results, as well as strategies to improve these. Once the project period ends, we will set aside an entire day a month dedicated to following up results, as well as for educational development.

Milestone 2: When the Teaching and Learning for All group is given responsibility as important actors with regard to project implementation and educational development at Høyenhall School

During the first year, a representative for each school section was chosen to participate in the project group. The group held a meeting prior to a visit from the supervisors in order to participate in planning, and participated in meetings with the supervisors as well. Prior to the second year we decided to increase the number of members in the group, and that we would change its name to the Pedagogical Development (PU) team, as we wanted to connect the project to the general educational/pedagogical development initiatives at the school. Later, we saw an increasing need to work with special education and specialized Norwegian teaching, so we expanded the group by adding two teachers from each section, one 'regular' teacher and one SEND teacher. Regular meeting periods were scheduled, the mandate was re-examined and the members were given more tasks than in the previous year, related to the contents of the core time and department-specific time, among other things. Throughout the year we have spent a great deal of time making improvements to the special education lessons and specialized Norwegian teaching, both with regard to contents and organization.

Element 2: Teaching and Learning

Milestone 1: When supervision through the use of observation sheets becomes a tool for improvement of teaching and learning

The staff began working on common educational standards at Høyenhall School as early as the first session with the Teaching and Learning for All coaches during the planning days in August 2013. In the period between August and the next visit at the end of September, they had agreed upon a standard; which we have called the observation sheet (see appendix). We had several Teach First candidates at the school, and the observation sheet was based on the planning sheet used in Teach First. During the autumn, criteria and characteristics on starting and ending were determined, as well as differentiation. The sheet has since been used by school leaders during observations.

To improve the leadership's observational and advising expertise, we invited external experts to a leadership meeting. One spent half a day with the leader group, and we received tips and advice on how to properly advise and supervise teachers. We recognize that it may be a while before all staff members feel comfortable about being filmed.

In order to aid the leadership in reaching a common understanding of what constitutes a good lesson with a maximal learning outcome, we carried out several observations with the coaches, before discussing what type of feedback could be given to each teacher. These observations have been highly useful, and they have greatly contributed to a common understanding. They have also helped the school leaders to practise observation and supervision in the same manner, with regard to both scope and methods. These mutual observations are something we have continued to utilize during the second year of the project. School leaders wish to continue mutual observations in the classroom also after the project is concluded.

Throughout the autumn of 2013, the staff stated that they wanted to try peer observation and supervision. This was implemented in the spring of 2014. The composition of pairs was discussed in the project group, and we decided to create a template wherein each pair would belong to the same department, while not necessarily teaching the same subject. This setup was evaluated before the summer, and during the school year 2014/15, time was allocated for peer observation and supervision in the individual working hour agreement. Evaluations indicated that this was successful, and we will therefore continue to utilize this system. During the evaluation of the observation and supervision system, many reported feeling uncomfortable about giving their co-workers direct feedback. We therefore carried out a separate session on supervision, whereby two experienced professional teachers explained the theory of supervision and provided tips and advice. We have noted that further supervision sessions will need to be carried out with the same pairs before the teachers feel comfortable with one another to the extent that they are able to offer constructive criticism.

After the first year a new milestone plan was developed; we determined that the school's primary focus areas during that school year would be differentiation, writing and special education/specialized Norwegian teaching.

Milestone 2: When we use results to ensure reading and math progression

The school had previously followed the trial Oslo plan, but lacked a complete overview of the various tests, and the need for 'practice tests' for the different years. Therefore, a local test plan was developed according to a general template for all years. With guidance from the coaches we have become more familiar with tools for 'tracking' students, and these have been partially adopted at the secondary level. For the primary years we still primarily use the national system 'VOKAL' to register and follow up results.

Milestone 3: When the sum of adaptive teaching, special education and specialized Norwegian teaching enables students' educational progression

Parallel to participation in the project, we have made significant changes in the organization of special education and specialized Norwegian teaching. The first change is that we now have dedicated teachers with a high level of expertise teaching these classes, and we have clearly defined the teachers' areas of responsibility. During the autumn of 2013, the so-called 20 per cent students in all years were identified. The premise here is that this group will not be permanent, but should instead be comprised of students who need extra attention and support, for various reasons, for a longer or shorter period. An overview of these students is discussed at team meetings, and the teachers agree on how to follow up these students.

During the spring term of 2014, the school participated in trying out '*Språkbroen*' ('The Language Bridge'), a collection of resources intended to assist in the teaching of students with minority-language backgrounds. One of the SEND teachers at the school tried a planning sheet, called the *focus sheet* at Høyenhall School, after some modifications were made. Filling out the focus sheet during the weekly team meeting is now mandatory. The SEND teachers and the other teachers will come together and plan the next period, in terms of topics, words and expressions, with regard to the students who may require something extra in that regard. Identifying the 20 per cent students and jointly planning the education for each class, with and without a SEND teacher, has led to entirely different attitudes among the staff with regard to students who have been identified as SEN; the perception is now that these students are *everyone*'s responsibility at all times.

Furthermore, we have been very fortunate this year to have a specialist teacher with a high level of expertise and knowledge on special education and specialized Norwegian teaching, and who has done a thorough job in charting the present situation. Along with the social service teacher, they have managed the special educators at the school, initiated work on forming a plan and a standard for special education, and participated in PU as well. While charting students, the specialist teacher observed many classes and smaller groups at the school in order to determine the type of education that works for the students. She has later given feedback to each individual team, and has presented her summary to the entire staff.

The plan is to focus on two teams over a period of two to three weeks. The specialist teacher will also participate in team meetings to hear how the teachers summarize the previous week, and on the basis of their experiences, and find out what they are planning for the following week.

Milestone 4: When work with school subjects and assessment contributes towards an improved learning outcome for each pupil

Høyenhall School has, like most other schools, regularly worked on developing a local curricula/teaching goals. We noted, however, that the relationship between these plans, the curricula, weekly schedules and assessments was insufficient. We therefore began working on this, and we will continue to give even more attention to assessment in the future. During the second term the teachers developed a set of marking symbols, as a standard for Høyenhall School, one for literacy and one to use in mathematics. They are still in use, but we need to work more on how to sustain using these symbols throughout the school.

There was never any doubt that a great deal of good work is being done at the school, and that many teachers plan and carry out excellent lessons for their students. However, not enough time has been allocated to the collaboration and sharing of good lessons. Therefore, this year we have emphasized sharing good lessons during core time, and during planning days/evenings. This has also been done with Teaching and Learning for All coaches present. We recognize that it is not always easy to attain strong cooperation between teachers, since they are not always present at the same time. This is why we have set aside an extra hour for cooperation in the working schedule agreement for the next school year, so that teachers can develop good lessons together.

Milestone 5: When emphasis on reading and writing in all subjects makes students better writers

The school already emphasized reading and mathematics, but it was clear that there was a continued need to focus on writing. We furthermore realized that these efforts could easily be implemented into the Teaching and Learning for All project, becoming a part of it instead of an addition. This was primarily a secondary school-level project, but we quickly decided to include Years 1–7 in the project. The project has been maintained in lectures at the University of Oslo (UiO), as well as under follow-up from UiO advisers at the school. Follow-up resources have been used for meetings with the leader group and PU, for two common staff meetings. The project will continue throughout 2015. During the autumn of 2015, we will focus on making a step-by-step writing plan, as well as to include the writing efforts in later educational assessment work.

Milestone 6: When adaptive teaching permeates all teaching and leads to mastery and development for each pupil

Milestone 6, just like Milestone 5 involving writing, was added to the plan starting in 2015. After many observations during the first year of the project, it became clear that there was a need to further develop teacher competency in the areas of differentiation and adaptive teaching. This is a broad field, and many teachers have said that they find it difficult to differentiate and vary their lessons to the extent that students are receiving adapted teaching.

We have therefore had several visits from the coach with regard to the topic of differentiation. We have worked with Bloom's taxonomy on two visits, and the teachers have, following the coach's examples and ideas, collaborated on differentiated educational plans. School work on educational walls has also been an important contribution to the efforts on improving differentiation. Many of the students, particularly the 20 per cent students, require and benefit greatly from some form of visual aid. Once the coach had held an introductory session on the topic, we worked using the coffee table method, and a number of suggestions arose. This has been the starting point for major efforts this spring, where each department has discussed and agreed on a 'lowest common denominator'. The plan is that we will begin outfitting classrooms and a number of common areas this autumn.

Throughout the past two years, we have of course given extra attention to the weakest 20 per cent students, according to our goals. At the same time, it has been important for us to safeguard the students on the other end of the scale. With that in mind, we invited an author and representative of the Association of Gifted Children to the school. This was viewed as a useful session, and work was followed up by teachers collaborating across stages to develop differentiated tasks that would see to the educational needs of all students. We have also had an extra focus on so-called 'rich tasks'. This has been particularly emphasized in mathematics, where teacher experience has been shared in meetings.

It would not be possible to complete measures to achieve differentiation and sufficient variation. We will continue our efforts to develop criteria for adaptive teaching and view this in conjunction with the evaluation of the observation sheet and the question, 'How do we know the students have learned?' With the transition to the new IT platform, 'It's learning', we will ensure the proper systems for storage, sharing and planning to ensure that teachers can make more effective use of good teaching material by others.

Element 3: Parent and carer engagement

Milestone 1: When structured conversations lead to a maximal learning outcome for each pupil

Structured conversations were the main topic during the second planning day in August 2013. This session had the following objectives:

- To understanding the purpose and nature of the structured conference

- To consider the basic skills of conducting a structured conference

- To consider some tools for setting objectives and overcoming obstacles

- To share ways of communicating with hard-to-reach parents.

In addition to a theoretical introduction, the staff was also given the opportunity to practise conference conversations through role play, using cases. All teachers were given suggestions for good questions that could be used during the conference conversations. Teachers were then given the task of completing structured conversations immediately after the start of the school year. Teachers were also given a new template for documentation of completed parent conferences, stating the goal of the conference. A new feature of the conference involved asking the parents to say something positive about their own child.

Milestone 2: When cooperation with parents contributes positively to the school's reputation

Høyenhall School has a complex and, to a certain extent, challenging parent group which demands quality and, quite rightly, asks questions about school operations and content. This is a small local community, and parents often speak to one another on a daily basis. The school has felt the need to work on improving its reputation. When commencing the project, we felt it was important to collaborate with the parents, and we decided to appoint a parent committee. The parent committee provided ideas and suggestions for the annual plan and for the content of the parent meetings.

The Parent Council Working Committee has found it difficult to get parents to join the council, so there has unfortunately been little continuity in this aspect. Few Parent Council meetings have been scheduled, but the school leaders have always been present at meetings.

There have been previous reports that some of the parent meetings have not been of sufficient quality, and that this is the reason many parents do not attend. We decided therefore, in cooperation with the Parent Council, that we would try to introduce a new structure for this school year. Each meeting will always be comprised of two parts: one for the entire year in the auditorium and with the school leaders in attendance, and one for each individual class. It was furthermore decided that the autumn meeting would include a half-hour gathering in the auditorium with information from the school leaders, but that the main part of the meeting would be held for each class. The spring meeting would include various topics, and the main part of the meeting would be for the entire pupil year, while a brief session would be held for each class. These topics would be held regularly, so that they would always be a meeting about Safe Learning for Year 1, Smart Internet Use for Year 2, Youth, Alcohol and Drugs for Year 8, and so on. In this manner we will ensure that all topics are covered and that the quality of the meetings improves. The Parent Council provided an evaluation of the first meeting this year, stating that the topic meetings were very good, but that the meetings held in the classrooms afterwards were too long and detailed. This is therefore something we would like to continue working on in the coming school year.

Element 4: Wider outcomes

Milestone 1: When cooperation between the school, parents and other agencies contributes towards improved learning outcomes, fewer absences and an environment free from bullying and violence

The staff has spent a good deal of time working on this area; this has largely dealt with competency enhancement and common understanding. But we feel this area needs further development. The school has traditionally enjoyed good cooperation with the police on the topic of prevention. Naturally a great deal of contact between the police and the school leaders has taken place without the attendance of the rest of the staff. This particularly applies to teachers of younger students. The police have visited the school during core hours and provided the opportunity to ask questions. In their evaluations, teachers stated that they found this to be positive. Representatives from public health and social services for young people (*utekontakten*) also attended these meetings, and presented their services.

A general annual plan for cooperation and shared information will be completed in the autumn of 2015. We have encountered difficulties in that several agencies do not attend extended resource team meetings, and would like the annual plan to be discussed there.

Impact

Element 1: Leadership

As a result of the Achievement for All programme, The Høyenhall leader group has strengthened its leadership: they are now dynamic, bold, reflective and strategic. They now have high expectations of staff and students alike. There is a changed culture towards more openness and professional trust. This can be seen through a number of new structures and measures:

Strategic leadership

The leader group at Høyenhall has become **strategic**. The head teacher and the leader group felt the need for a plan which allowed for forensic monitoring and evaluation and a clear line of responsibility and thus accountability. This 'milestone plan' adhered to the Four Elements of the Achievement for All framework and closely guided the reconfigured leader group in their governance. The existence of a detailed plan offered a framework for school improvement rather than relying on custom and practice. It also ensured that leaders did not falter in the face of resistance. The milestones were also quantifiable. The plan was also the focal point for the sessions with the coach.

As a result of the programme, the leader group has increased the amount of **meetings** in the planned schedule. The head teacher has used staff meetings to roll out and seek staff views. Høyenhall has used **meetings** as an integral part of the implementation of developments. They increase opportunity for consistency and ensure a more rapid response to strategies.

Change management

The Achievement for All framework has afforded the leader group the mandate and structure to manage significant **change** with the partnership of the staff. To this end, it has

- **consulted** with whole staff when making significant changes or devising key policies, such as standards for 'the good lesson', the introduction of formal observations and standards for the learning environment. The changes have not been 'top-down.'

- included and **negotiated** with the union regarding changes which may impact on teaching schedules and workload.

- created and formalized dedicated **extra time.**

- **remunerated** some staff for taking on additional responsibilities.

- for **transparency** and extended governance, the head teacher and Achievement for All coaches introduced the Achievement for All programme to key **stakeholders** – the school board (DS) and parent group (FAU). Student leaders were also central to this.

- fostered **cohesion** and more **unity** in realization that the hitherto factious staff was a barrier to introducing change.

'Distributed' leadership

The head teacher has enhanced or created new roles. Some have added capacity, while others bring an expertise hitherto missing. An example of this has been the deployment of an ex- head teacher to lead and coordinate interventions for students vulnerable to underachievement: SEND, SNO, problems at home. Other examples of 'distributed' leadership are the AfA group (PU). All teaching and learning developments such as differentiation, observations and the learning environment have been routed through this 'pedagogic' forum. The head teacher has developed the ability to spot, encourage and manage talent. This has proved to empower staff, ensure buy-in and further the development of the Achievement for All changes.

Accountability and quality assurance

The leader group has established practices to ensure **accountability** and **quality** assurance. Staff have been receptive to training and monitoring. Colleagues have engaged and some actively encouraged and welcomed this level of scrutiny and evaluation. The leader group also conducts annual performance interviews. This device can be further used to hold teachers accountable for raising standards and to embed pedagogic strategies.

Strong and mindful

The leadership measures have evoked an increasing trust, professional respect and confidence in the leader group. Leadership is increasingly strong. It is measured, informed and strategic. Therefore, the development of the Høyenhall leadership has been a real success of the project.

Element 2: Good teaching and learning

Leaders had recognized the need for teachers to improve their practice through a structured, developmental approach to teaching focused on improving pupil learning.

Good teaching and learning – Use of data to drive student progress

At the start of the Year 2 of the Achievement for All programme, the leaders for grades 3 and 9 presented 2014 data, comparing it to 2013. This began the year with high expectations, and

- established baselines for numeracy and reading
- discerned gaps between the whole year grade and the AfA cohort
- revealed underachievement of more able students
- analysed the nature of the tests (test same in Years 7 and 8 so students should have performed better but easier to compare)
- noted skills/questions that needed a greater focus, for example, reading a greater concern for Year 3.

In response, the leader group developed the following strategies:

- a school-based 'Test plan' to practise and drill the students in preparation for external tests

- started building individual contextual data to start to explain underachievement and low attainment: emotional and special need. This was the start of a provision map

- built on the above, devised interventions

- appointed an ex-head teacher to develop above the teacher and learning plan.

Good teaching and learning: Raising standards in the classroom (Pedagogy)

Høyenhall has taken a laser light focus on pedagogy. This is where most of the developments have occurred. The Achievement for All coach worked closely with the leader group to develop strategies to lift standards in the classroom: clear characteristics of excellent teaching with mechanisms to know the situation and to further drive up standards.

Developing the Høyenhall standards

This followed the coach-led discussion of what constitutes a good lesson. The leader group led a series of meetings with the staff and phase representatives. These meetings encouraged the staff to discuss academic thought and consider evidence. The result was a comprehensive list of standards/competencies under four main headings. They provided the shape for an excellent lesson. The headings were:

- General expectations of the teacher – covering expectations such as lesson structure and mode of communication

- Start of the lesson including learning outcomes

- During the lesson (learning activities) – this is the heart of the lesson with an expectation that a variety of activities is used, different modes of assessment and a positive ethos

- The end of the lesson – a clear summing up and setting of homework.

This sheet became the centralized format used by leaders to observe. As these standards were developed in partnership, there is an expectation that teachers follow them. This single format drew on the best practice around student motivation and engagement. It also made reference to differentiation with mention of attending to the students' needs. Introducing a single format was new and constituted a cultural shift away from proliferation and laissez-faire towards consistency and alignment.

Quality assurance and monitoring

To embed the above and to ensure consistency, the leader group worked alongside the Achievement for All coach to raise standards and to ensure quality teaching. They used peer 'mutual' and leader group observations and thematic learning walks. The coaches ran a series of sessions on how to observe and how to give quality feedback to the staff by using a coaching model. This drew on the good practice from the English Ofsted guidance and the training materials from ASCL, the head teachers union in the UK. As a result, Høyenhall developed its own observation sheet that captured the key areas of the lesson standards. The leader group were keen to use observations for both development and evaluation. This was the subject of several forthright and challenging discussions with the coaches:

- What is the key purpose of the observation?
- How would observations happen?
- How would the findings be used?
- Would the peer observations use the leader group format?
- Would the peer observations e recorded centrally?
- Who would choose the pairs?

As a result of the programme, Høyenhall uses a range of quality assurance strategies: learning walks and lesson observations. Staff are more open about being visited and see the value of being held to account.

Provision mapping and interventions

To provide expertise and to add capacity, an ex-head teacher coordinated SEND and SNO and worked alongside the social worker, to create provision maps: identifying students, barriers, devising interventions upskilling staff through thematic (SEND) observations. As a result of the Achievement for All framework, Høyenhall has gone some way with a laser light focus on the vulnerable learners. These interventions exist within the growing SEND and SNO provision. As good practice would dictate, the most powerful strand of this is the universal provision. In other words, adapting teaching to meet the needs of all the students. There is now a shared responsibility towards the bottom 20 per cent of the school community. Data shows that the rate of progress of these students is better than those without additional needs.

Differentiation

The Høyenhall leader group built differentiation into their Milestone Plan, monitored against progress among all pupils, 'when adaptive teaching permeates all teaching and leads to mastery and development for each pupil'. It was added to reflect their focus on pedagogy and an attempt to acknowledge the need for accelerated progress for students, particularly the bottom 20 per cent and those at the other end of the ability spectrum. The Høyenhall leader group made differentiation a key focus of the raising of lesson standards. They carried out themed learning walks and are now intensifying observations to specifically audit the SEND and SNO provision. Differentiation is now an expectation. It is a key component of a 'good' lesson. There is a realization that every student has an entitlement to make continual progress and staff have a duty to ensure it.

The developments in differentiation have been further embedded by the appointment of expert SEND and SNO teachers. They have been central to planning, differentiating and identifying and teaching smaller targeted groups. This paradigm of 'plan, do and review' with the use of prior attainment data, is also being used to identify and target the more able students.

The learning environment

As part of the raising standards in the classroom, Høyenhall was keen to improve the conditions of the learning environment. The Achievement for All coach ran an evening workshop for the whole staff, entitled 'Learning Walls – Using the environment for learning'. The training explored the intellectual, emotional and physical purpose of stimulating displays, and the central role that the environment has in promoting the following:

- ethos
- key/basic skills – literacy, numeracy, ICT
- learning strategies
- subject knowledge
- assessment criteria – at different levels
- corridors
- aesthetics

The planning for the training was illustrative of distributed and democratic leadership. Each table explored one of the above themes. Every member of staff had to contribute to every table/theme. This approach was to challenge directly staff who were very silent in staff-wide discussions. We also built in time for teams to create and decide what are the key terms, concepts and skills to display in their classroom, using the principles shared by our Achievement for All coach.

Assessment, marking and feedback
Work has started on common practice with the introduction of marking symbols across the school. The leader group is aware that there is not enough timely feedback to the students. The Achievement for All coach suggested that the differentiation strategies will be strengthened by a robust, specific and directional assessment policy. Along with the strategic work with data, the leader group team will develop assessment next academic year.

Element 3: Parent and carer engagement

The Structured Conversation

Høyenhall has worked with the coach to increase parent and carer engagement. The key strategy has been the development of the structured conversations. The coach followed the Achievement for All prescribed structure for training, which gives ample opportunities to rehearse the different components of the structured conversation. There were concerns about where and how the structured conversations would embed at Høyenhall. Rather than being a strategy for only the AfA cohort, all students at Høyenhall receive a 'conference' using structured conversation principles.

Høyenhall School's plans to engage parents are becoming more strategic. Research tells us that there is a strong correlation between good parental engagement and high academic success.

Element 4: Wider outcomes

'When the co-operation between the school, parents and other stakeholders contribute to improved outcomes, less absenteeism and an environment free of harassment and violence'

(Milestone Plan)

The leader group of Høyenhall acknowledges the importance of partnership work with local external agencies, such as police, social service/child protection and health services. This is key to having a holistic view of keeping students safe. All agencies have visited the school in a special public relations capacity.

The school has an anti-bullying strategy, with students playing an active role. Students' perception is that there is still bullying. The school will have to strengthen its behaviour policy and actively challenge bullying and the student's perceptions about feeling safe.

The leader group of Høyenhall has focused its efforts on element 2 – good teaching and learning. The Achievement for All coach led a residential course focusing on strategies and systems for inclusion. This can be built on to further develop a positive behaviour management system. Once the teaching and learning starts to embed, then the leadership team can turn to strengthening the wider outcomes that clearly impact on student success.

Summary

Høyenhall's participation in the Achievement for All programme has been powerful. The school has established new systems and procedures to support raising standards; there is a changed culture around wanting to improve teaching. After their initial concerns about embarking on another project, the staff are now more behind the leader group and the Achievement for All programme. Each of the developments have gained momentum as they are embedded into regular practice. There is also a growing culture of collaboration. This change is largely due to the head teacher and reconfigured leader group's strategic and forensic, mindful and tenacious approach. There is a growth mindset by the staff and increasingly for the students. The leader group has fostered 'reflexive' practice. Such reflection and the desire to improve outcomes for the students and to strengthen teacher skills have meant the engagement with the latest academic research, training and best practice. Solutions to underachievement now lie not in the home or in the community but in the school, particularly the classroom. Due to such structural and cultural change, Høyenhall is well poised for transformation.
As the school principal stated:

> For the school leader it has been especially important that Teaching and Learning for All should not be something outside ordinary school operations, but rather something that permeates the organisation and its daily operations. We believe that this has been successful to a large extent. When the project period is over we will therefore not be ending these measures or decreasing our focus on the 20% weakest students, but rather continue to act and think as an 'Achievement for All' school in the years to come.

Recommendations

The Achievement for All programme has signalled a shift in culture at both Lindeberg and Høyenhall schools. There are monumental changes in attitudes and processes in leadership and pedagogy. There is an understanding of the impact of contextual factors to **explain** but not excuse low attainment and underachievement. To this end, teachers have engaged with training, joint planning, evaluation and partnership with other schools. The schools have embraced these developments and are well poised for even deeper, wider and sustained transformation.

Recommendations

1   Continue with an annual needs analysis

2   Provide all staff with Achievement for All training

3   Extend structured conversation approach across all schools

4   Consider implications of adopting Achievement for All in all Oslo schools

5   Consider introducing the Achievement for All early years' programme, Achieving Early, in early years and primary settings.

The following chapter moves the focus from teaching and learning to parental engagement. The involvement of John Hopkins University and the GEMS parental engagement team expanded the knowledge of the Achievement for All coaches and those engaged in developing the project in the United States.

PART FIVE

Why School Environments and Parental Engagement Need to Change

CHAPTER TEN

The US Context: Engaging the Parents of Pupils Identified with SEND

The most accurate predictor of a student's achievement in school is not income or social status, but the extent to which that student's family is able to create a home environment that encourages learning; communicate high, yet reasonable, expectations for their children's achievement and future careers; and become involved in their children's education at school and in the community.

(SCHARGEL AND SMINK, 2001)

Never has there been such a strong focus on parental engagement in children's learning. The evidence from the international base shows a strong association between parental support of children's education and their academic achievement (Desforges and Abouchaar, 2003; O' Brien and Shemilt, 2003; Harris and Goodall, 2007; Goodall et al., 2011, Gorard, Huat See and Davies, 2012; OECD, 2011). This is also reflected in government policy and the wider research literature. For example, since 1987, Joyce Epstein's six-part typology has supported many schools in developing effective parent engagement strategies.

Surprisingly, however, many parents do not realize that they have a part in their children's learning. This puts greater burden on schools to find effective ways to involve them; this can take varying forms with varying degrees of impact. Examples of parents supporting children's learning include at home – through homework, talking to them, reading to them; at school – volunteering in school and attending parents' evenings and school–home partnerships – where traditionally parents engage in their children's learning by holding meetings with teachers to discuss their children and aspirations for their children, by setting targets and by conducting parent–child learning-together programmes. But how effective are these as mechanisms for real parental engagement in children's learning? For schools, 'getting it right' for learners with high needs and their parents, requires careful consideration as to what is meant by parental support. This chapter will consider parental support of children's learning and how this can be effectively developed by and through schools.

Defining parental support

A review of the literature highlights the complexity in either clearly defining parental support or in 'distilling' the effect from other variables. Parameters are frequently set by the researchers with the result that measurement of parental involvement and parental engagement is subjective; this is generally explored through parental support within the context of either parental involvement or parental engagement. Frequently, both terms are used interchangeably, where neither term is clearly defined. Gorard et al. (2012) in their review of related literature cite 'parent as teacher and parent-school alignment' as the two principal mechanisms through which parental involvement impacts on children's attainment. Harris and Goodall (2007: 38–68), on the other hand, highlight the nature of parental engagement, which 'is not about engaging with the school, but with the learning of the child' and where 'engagement implies that parents are an essential part of the learning process, an extended part of the pedagogic process'. This holistic view of parental engagement provided by Harris and Goodall (2007) reflects the Parent Engagement Partnership Program (PEPP) model in New York and that of the Achievement for All framework implemented across schools in England.

Parental involvement versus parental engagement

Catsambis (2001) explored the link between parental involvement practices and the educational outcomes of high school seniors. Data was drawn from the National Educational Longitudinal Study (NELS: 88), a study exploring student progress from eighth grade through to work. Using studies from 1988 (Base year) and 1992 (second follow-up year), the only initial years parental data was included, Catsambis employed data from 13,580 parents and their children. Using factor analysis to identify parent indices in line with Epstein's (1992, 1995) parameters for parental involvement, different indices were employed for eighth and twelfth grade parental involvement. Various socio-economic factors and other demographic characteristics were controlled.

Findings showed that parental involvement in the eighth grade has little or no impact on student achievement growth during high school. Parental expectations and encouragement for college have the highest positive association with student achievement. Findings further showed that a very strong link in the context of parental involvement is that between parental monitoring of coursework and student achievement. Findings showed that when parents monitored their children's coursework in high school, students achieved more credits in English and science.

In England, employing data from the National Child Development Study (NCDS), a longitudinal study of children born in the UK in one week in March 1958, Hango (2007) explored mother and father involvement on children's academic outcomes. The original data in the NCDS included 17,000 mothers (98 per cent of births that week) with follow-up interviews at age 7, 11, 16, 23 and 42. Employing a two-phased approach, Hango considered the link between children from disadvantaged families and education at age seven and father and mother involvement at age eleven. The second phase considered the same variables at sixteen years. In the final instance, with various restrictions imposed on the data by the researcher, the sample included data from 3,072 participants in phase one and 2,658 in phase two.

In measuring parental involvement at age eleven, Hango considered both teacher assessment of parental involvement and parent perception of their involvement; the latter focused on frequency of child–parent outings. For phase two he considered parental involvement in the context of how well the child and parent 'got on' (child perception). Overall findings showed that parental involvement of both the mother and the father was greater for parents with higher qualifications. In addition, although outings with the mother and father's interest in education had a positive impact on future qualifications, father's social class, living in an owner-occupied house, child's gender, behaviour and reading ability, were the most relevant indicators of later achievement (as measured by future qualifications).

In the Netherlands, Kloosterman et al. (2011) explored parental reading socialization and school involvement on children's attainment and progress during primary school. Drawing data from the Dutch Cohort Study Primary Education (PRIMA), a biennial study examining the cognitive ability and social skills of Dutch primary school children, the researchers considered data for 11,916 second grade pupils (5–6 years) in 587 primary schools. Data provided details on family social status and pupil language and maths performance in grades 2, 4, 6 and 8 for school years 1996/7, 1998/9, 2000/1 and 2002/3. Attrition was approximately 20 per cent at each measurement point, with the greatest attrition among disadvantaged children.

Researchers measured parental involvement through four indicators: frequency with which parents spoke to their child about school-related issues (parental data); frequency with which parents attended school meetings (parental data); the extent to which parents had good contact with the school (teacher data); and the extent they were actively involved with the school (teacher data). Findings showed that both parental school involvement and parental reading socialization have an impact on children's language development; the impact on maths achievement was not strong. Findings further showed that over the course of primary schooling, the effect of early parental reading instruction had a positive impact on children's language performance.

De Fraja et al. (2010) explored the impact of parental, teacher and pupil effort on child's achievement. Employing data from the British NCDS, the researchers measured the child's effort through his/her attitude (e.g. what he/she thinks of school), parental effort through their interest in their child's education (e.g. frequency of reading to child, attendance at school meetings) and teacher effort through their perception of school's involvement with parent (e.g. does the school initiate contact/involvement with parents). Findings showed a multiplier effect in parent–child effort; that is, the researchers found that parental effort 'induces' the child to make more effort, which pleases the parent, etc. Interestingly, their findings further showed that schools have a positive response to children's effort, but not to parents.

Flouri and Buchanan (2004) explored the role of the father's and mother's involvement in their child's later attainment. The roles were considered independently. Drawing data from the National Child Development Study in the UK, on 3,303 individuals which had details of father's involvement at age seven, mother's involvement at age seven and qualifications on leaving school by the age of twenty. Measures of involvement included reading to the child, going on outings with the child, taking an interest in the child's education and father managing the child. Findings suggested that father and mother involvement at age seven predicted educational attainment by age twenty. In highlighting weaknesses in the data the researchers refer to the greater attrition of disadvantaged children over the years.

Flouri (2006) considered, among other issues, the impact of mother and fathers' interest in their child's education on educational attainment by age 26. Taking into account various socio-economic factors, the findings showed that mother's interest was closely associated with educational attainment in both men and women. Findings further showed that for women, father's interest in education positively impacted on their later educational attainment; for men, father's interest indirectly impacted, by increasing mother's involvement. The researcher concluded that parental interest had an impact on later educational attainment, but this relationship was stronger for women than men.

In the United States, Topor et al. (2010) explored how parental involvement increases pupil academic performance. Employing a sample of 158 children aged seven years, their mothers and their teachers, the researchers found a statistically significant association between parental involvement and a child's achievement; this was found to be over and above that of the child's intelligence. Participants were from three different groups, participating in a larger longitudinal study and included a cross-section of children (social and ethnic background). Various standard measuring instruments were used to assess parental involvement, relationship between student and teacher, children's cognitive and physical competence, along with peer and mother social acceptance and children's academic performance.

In considering the mechanism for parental involvement on child achievement, Topor et al. (2010) found that parental involvement positively impacts on the child's perception of his/her cognitive competence and on the student–teacher relationship. The researchers concluded that these factors contributed to increased academic performance in the children, where the parent engagement lead to increased achievement test scores for the child, while better student–teacher relationships resulted in higher academic performance in the classroom.

Nye et al. (2006) in their systematic review of research related to parental involvement and academic performance of elementary school children in the United States, employed stringent criteria in the identification of research for inclusion in the study. Defining parental involvement as 'the active engagement of a parent with their child outside of the school day in an activity which centres on enhancing academic performance', they conclude that parental involvement has a 'significant' impact on children's academic performance.

Summary of findings

It is clear that the research provides evidence for improved academic outcomes for children when their parents become engaged and involved in the process. In practical terms, the evidence suggests quite simple practices: parents showing an interest in their child's learning (De Fraja et al., 2010), which has a multiplier effect, and parents having high expectations and encouraging their children (Catsambis, 2001). In addition, the evidence highlights the relevance of early parental interaction having a longer-term impact on children's future qualifications and the better involvement of parents with higher qualifications (Hango, 2007). Topor et al. (2010) in the United States give consideration to the mechanism through which parental involvement and engagement works in the child – first by increasing the child's confidence in their own competencies and second by improving the child–teacher relationship.

What this means for schools

Too many high-needs children and young people are not achieving as well as their peers, relative to their starting points. These students are more likely to be excluded socially, suffer from bullying and have fewer friendships. Too many children are leaving school without the necessary skills that prepare them to become independent adults and world citizens in an increasingly competitive global environment. The PEPP model developed by Achievement for All in the UK and GEMS USA is designed to support schools in providing the best opportunities to ensure that all students make accelerated progress. It creates opportunities to link home and school on a number of levels to support student learning. Students take responsibility for their own learning and are determined to achieve, so they can lead full and successful lives. Schools that report better relationships between parents, teachers and schools see improved student attendance and significant reductions in bullying and behavioural problems.

This is particularly important for high-needs students, who are likely to face many challenges. The Alliance for Excellent Education in the publication 'Students with Disabilities in U.S. High Schools19', found that 'only 7% of eighth graders with disabilities scored at or above proficient on the National Assessment of Educational Progress in reading, compared to 31% of eighth graders without disabilities. ... Students with disabilities are five times less likely to enter postsecondary education than their peers. ... Almost three quarters of students identified as having emotional disturbances have been suspended or expelled.' Some families of high-needs students and especially of those with disabilities may still be going through what can be seen as a 'grieving process' well into their child's high school years. It is difficult for some parents to accept that their child faces challenges to learning and achievement. The Collaborative Conversation used in PEPP can support parents to understand the implications of their child's disability and be informed about how the school can help the student and the parents to move forward. The Annie E. Casey Foundation publication 'Why Equal Opportunity is Important' clearly stated the long-term consequences of 'failing to ensure educational success': 'The adverse impact is long term and reflected in future employment prospects, poverty and incarceration rates, as well as limited capacity to participate in the world community.'

Research demonstrates that parents are more likely to participate in their child's education when they feel welcomed and connected to the school and their child's teachers (Ellis and Hughes, 2002). This has implications for schools in terms of developing welcoming environments and a 'welcome' culture for all members of the school community. Schools are perceived as more inviting when they display acceptance of different parent cultures and customs (Ortiz, Robertson and Wilkinson, 2009). When parents are valued they will have a greater willingness to become involved in the school (Constantino, 2003). There is a consistent correlation between improving the quality of parent's engagement with their child's school and improved rates of attendance, behaviour and achievement. The gains are often most significant where schools are newly able to engage parents who were previously considered difficult to engage or 'hard to reach'.

The barriers that schools face in engaging all parents and carers can be a result of deeply rooted socio-economic or other factors. Recent research (The Annie E. Casey Foundation, 2010) found that on a state-by-state basis across the United States, between 22 per cent and 39 per cent of all children are living in households where no parent has full-time, year-round employment. For the children and young people themselves, these barriers can have extensive impacts on their ambition, access and achievement. The research paper 'Latinos and Education: Explaining the Attainment Gap' presented by Mark Hugo Lopez to the 2009 Latino Children, Families, and Schooling National Conference concluded that 'the biggest reason for the gap between the high value Latinos place on education and their more modest ambitions to finish college appears to come from financial pressure to support a family. … Nearly three-quarters (74%) of all 16 to 25-year-old survey respondents who cut their education short during or right after high school say they did so because they had to support their family.'

Essentially, clear leadership of parent engagement will bring about real change and improve the ambitions, access and achievement of all students and their families.

Effective leaders find appropriate ways to overcome the obstacles to parental engagement; including time, resources, and assumptions (including assumptions about what parents are able and willing to contribute to their children's education). Leaders know and understand the context of their school. Research is clear; parent engagement is a key factor in raising attainment and achievement, where effective parent engagement lies in

> specific school programs and teacher practices that encourage parent involvement at school and guide parents in how to help their children at home.
>
> (Epstein and Dauber)

For high-needs students, good schools know that perhaps the most important thing is for them to be able to experience success at some level every day – whether that success is in reading, writing or maths at their own level, or in sports, performing arts or being a good friend. Engaging and understanding the views and experiences and ambitions of parents are key factors in recognizing and celebrating those successes. For example: Ben is in junior high and has spent much of his time working at RTI Tier 3. Despite all this effort he is still falling further behind the other students and his behaviour is getting worse. His teachers feel that they had done everything possible for him and that the only remaining alternative is for Ben to transfer to a different school. At Ben's first Collaborative Conversation, his parents told the teacher how scared he was of changing schools and losing his friends. The teacher is now taking advice from a psychologist and the school special needs teacher. These professional conversations are designed to explore ways in which Ben can stay in the classroom for most of the day and how to train a small number of his friends as peer mentors to work with him on a rota.

These interventions are planned to quickly improve Ben's motivation and to help him make rapid gains in reading and math. His English teacher is designing a series of interventions that his parents will be able to use at home.

Personalized, more individual solutions will be used where other small-group programmes or one-to-one support have not been effective. Such solutions are likely to include seeking specialist professional advice from outside the school. Parents and families should be involved in identifying these solutions, and (where appropriate) implementing them.

Parent engagement in schools helps students have access to everything that school has to offer to help them learn. Often, the first thing we think about when we think of 'access' is a ramp for wheelchair-users or Braille signage for students who are blind or visually impaired. Working with parents and families (and listening to their ambitions and experiences) to make sure physical access is good is, of course, important, but it is only part of ensuring 'access'. True equity means giving all students access to the full programme of study and to high-quality teaching and learning as a matter of entitlement. When a student struggles for any reason, it is essential that the teacher, the student and the parents consider the reasons for the barrier to learning rather than assuming that the child is lacking ability.

An increasing body of research evidence identifies that the quality of parent engagement makes a positive difference to student learning and achievement. The National Parent Teacher Association stated that high-quality parent engagement leads to

- higher student achievement 'regardless of socioeconomic status, ethnic/racial background, or the parents' education level', and

- improved achievement for disadvantaged students who 'can reach levels that are standard for middle-class children. In addition, the children who are farthest behind make the greatest gains.'

A 2002 University of Michigan research digest quotes Williams and Chavkin (1989) in stating, 'The more parents participate in schooling, in a sustained way, at every level – in advocacy, decision-making and oversight roles, as fund-raisers and boosters, as volunteers and paraprofessionals, and as home teachers – the better for student achievement.'

Summary

When schools support the engagement and commitment of parents to their child's learning and development in school, the rewards for both the child and the family are greater. For children and young people from poor families or those who are vulnerable to underachievement, they are more likely to participate in school and community life; the gap in achievement between themselves and their peers is likely to be narrowed and the students develop a clear idea of what good progress is for them.

The following chapter describes the PEPP, co-developed by the Achievement for All and GEMs teams to engage parents in improving their child's educational progress and outcomes.

CHAPTER ELEVEN

Improving Outcomes for SEND Through Parental Engagement: The Parent Engagement Partnership Program (PEPP)

Parental involvement in education is pivotal for the success of children throughout their school years and beyond.

(OECD, 2012)

The Parent Engagement Partnership Program (PEPP) is a collaboration between the UK charity, Achievement for All and GEMS USA, designed to support schools in providing the best opportunities to ensure that all students make accelerated progress. The programme began as a pilot in spring 2013 with schools in New York City. The particular model identifies high-needs students as the priority group of students but all programme elements are applicable to the whole-school population. The programme provides schools with support and resources from which they can develop sustainable local solutions to meet the needs of this group of students and the diverse range of families.

The programme aims to

- establish effective partnerships between teachers and families of students with high needs (the model identifies high-needs students as the priority group of students, but all programme elements are applicable to the whole-school population).

- foster development of positive relationships between students with high needs, their families, teachers and other professionals.

- provide development of parent engagement in a collaborative way that includes CPD.

- create an environment where all students are listened to and their opinions valued.

- implement effective and lasting engagement routines with families.

- create a welcoming school environment.

This chapter will consider the programme and how it is implemented and developed in schools to raise aspirations and increase access leading to improved achievement trajectories for children and young people.

Introduction

PEPP might be defined through a single goal, that of supporting schools working with teachers to increase the aspirations, access and achievement of all students by improving the quality of parent engagement and home–school partnerships. PEPP is a framework, developed and implemented in schools over two years. It takes an evidence-based approach to maximizing parent engagement in their children's education by focusing the school's leadership on parent engagement and by creating a 'custom-built' series of interventions that include and engage families and the community. Through the programme, schools are supported to develop a whole-school, strategic approach to parent engagement.

In essence, it provides an opportunity for schools to reflect and build on current practices approaching the development of parent engagement in a collaborative way that includes professional development for staff. PEPP schools not only raise parent and family ambitions about what their child can achieve but also encourage parents and families to engage with the school community, become more positive about what their child achieves, and more willing to celebrate all kinds of success – even small or incremental achievements.

The programme in practice

At the core of PEPP are two programme modules: 'Welcoming Families' (designed to engage families and the community in creating welcoming schools and positive learning environments) and 'The Collaborative Conversation' (designed to ensure that all teachers have the skills to engage with parents and families to improve student outcomes). In practice, these are implemented and developed in schools through a collaborative process including:

- up to twelve coaching visits each year from a PEPP coach who is an experienced professional;

- support for the PEPP school champion who leads the initiative in each school;

- targeted professional development in parent engagement for teachers, leaders and other staff through workshops and staff meetings;

- access to a range of parent engagement strategies to raise student aspiration, access and achievement; and

- evidence-based guidance on improving parent engagement.

The 'Welcoming Families' module builds on research that demonstrates that parents are more likely to participate in their child's education when they feel welcomed and connected to the school and their child's teachers (Ellis and Hughes, 2002). Parents, teachers and other stakeholders are invited to participate in a review of the school environment and culture for the level of 'welcome' it offers to all members of the school community. The review is an opportunity for schools to examine how family-friendly they are to parents and other community stakeholders.

Because PEPP is a tailored programme, the focus of the review will vary from school to school, but it is important that benchmarks are established that align with internationally developed parent engagement standards (GEMS School Standards Framework). The following Figure 11.1 shows how this process works in practice:

The process enables schools to address a vital first step in developing home–school collaboration. That is, through the opportunity for dialogue and understanding between the various stakeholders, including the students, a new outlook for changing the culture develops; this incorporates professional staff, parents and the community.

The 'Collaborative Conversations' module is also a key part of the programme in raising student aspiration, access and achievement. A dialogue starts between teachers and families that is focused on nurturing

FIGURE 11.1 *Parental Engagement Standards*

relationships, developing collaborative learning and raising student aspiration, access and achievement. Including students and families as equal members in supporting learning at home and in school is particularly important in the case of students with high needs. For example, 'For students with disabilities, improving a student's Individual Educational Plan by engaging families as active participants – focusing on establishing baselines; prioritizing measurable goals and assessing progress objectively – has been shown to have a positive impact on student achievement' (Bateman and Herr, 2006). The same is almost certainly true with other high-needs groups, particularly English language learners, where the dividends of collaborative learning are likely to be enriched by meeting the diverse needs of the whole family in many cases.

Mapp (2003) has suggested that 'if collaborative learning is to be achieved then all families must feel respected, and their voices truly heard in a setting that is welcoming and non-threatening'. She refers to this scenario as the 'joining process'. The joining process consists of three components: welcoming, honouring and connecting. Gonzalez and Moll (2002) have suggested that this is achieved through semi-collaborative interviews that are more conversational and in which both families and teachers learn from each other's perspective and about each other's context. In this second foundational module, the coach provides teachers with the tools and strategies through professional development that enable them to engage in a genuinely Collaborative Conversation with a student's parents.

Once the foundation module training is complete, the energy and the new professional skills of the teachers may be targeted to a number of additional interventions that build on and complement the PEPP foundation modules.

The first visit: School leaders, the PEPP coach and the PEPP school champion

Working in a collaborative way with parents to maximize parent engagement can be daunting and challenging for even the most experienced school leaders.

The PEPP coach provides support and advice to enable the school leaders and the school to implement the PEPP. As PEPP is a framework rather than a linear programme, the PEPP coach works closely with school leaders and their colleagues to develop the framework around the good practices currently taking place in the school. The PEPP coach supports improvements in the school, provides professional development for the PEPP school champion and colleague teachers, acts as an advocate for students and families, and supports and challenges the school's PEPP Welcoming Families group.

The initial meeting between the school leaders and the PEPP coach is an opportunity for both to provide context for the process of beginning to identify the school's priorities and requirements. School leaders often find it useful to ask some questions before and during the initial meeting with the PEPP coach. These initial questions can provide a framework for reference on a weekly basis; they can be a helpful way of tracking progress and a reassurance that things are happening.

Leading family engagement in partnership

Over the past two decades, a fundamental change has been taking place in schools around the world. In many countries, this change has seen a shift in the role of administrators from managing schools ('building administrators') to leading schools ('instructional leaders'). The international research evidence on this shift agrees: effective school leadership has a positive impact on the aspiration, access and achievement of children and their families, including those who live in difficult circumstances and those with a special need or a disability. Darling-Hammond et al. (2007) stress on 'the importance of developing a generation of strong, skilled leaders who can create schools that provide expert teaching for all students in settings where they can succeed'. Similarly, Pashiardis and Brauckmann (2009) note that 'there is increasing recognition of the importance of school leadership in supporting change and providing for educational quality. In fact, school leadership has been identified by a number of researchers as a key element in the effectiveness of school organizations.'

Effective and change-making PEPP school leaders employ their leadership skills to provide teaching and an environment that enables students and their parents to overcome the barriers they face referring to aspiration, access and achievement. These barriers can be multiple, and are often overlapping. They can include: learning needs; physical or mental disabilities; attention disabilities; social and socio-economic factors; cultural factors relating, for example, to race or gender; and resource factors such as the availability of specialized professional support or appropriate learning materials, or the timing of the school day.

Leading parent engagement

Leading parent engagement is the key element of PEPP. It is supported by the core modules of the programme – the Collaborative Conversation and Welcoming Families. Within PEPP, the leadership of parent engagement is fundamental to the overall themes of aspiration, access and achievement. These themes are underpinned and facilitated by three interrelated leadership behaviours: collaboration, communication and commitment. These behaviours lie at the heart of raising the aspirations, access and achievement of students, families, teachers and schools, and inform the PEPP approach to all aspects of parent engagement, including the Collaborative Conversations, the Welcoming Families module and other interventions such as learning behaviour tools or home–school visits.

Collaboration

School leaders encourage meaningful collaborations with families, most visibly through the Collaborative Conversations and the Welcoming Families. As part of this collaboration, successful school leaders are also 'outward facing'; they look beyond their own school to share experiences and practice, and to seek out new opportunities to forge partnerships.

Communication

Successful school leaders effectively communicate the importance of ambition, share their beliefs and celebrate success with students, families and colleagues in their own and other schools, and with other relevant agencies or professionals. Quality communications contribute to leading parent engagement by establishing two-way channels of communication based on mutual trust and respect, by ensuring that parent concerns and views are recognized and acted upon, and by providing feedback, data and celebrations of success.

Commitment

The school leaders' commitment to raising the ambition of all students encourages parents to aim high in their expectations, and is a vital foundation for the leading of parent engagement.

Leading parent engagement for aspiration – aiming high

Leading parent engagement in PEPP builds on a coherent and strategic vision of commitment, collaboration and communication to increase the ambition of parents and children through collaborative relationships. The PEPP framework for leading parent engagement is based on

- a strong vision and culture of genuine commitment, collaboration and communication with families, students, teachers and other school leaders
- strong values that are shared with all stakeholders

- professional development for school professionals in engaging families

- a belief in the entitlement of students and parents to high ambitions

- a willingness to listen and learn from the students and their families

- improving parent understanding of barriers to learning, and

- supporting parents by providing strategies to help their children learn more effectively.

Leading parent engagement for access– removing the barriers

One of the key ways that PEPP makes a difference to the lives of children and their families is through improving access to education and the wider opportunities and extracurricular activities the school can offer. The school leader puts into place systems, processes, partnerships and professional behaviours designed to improve families' access to: the school itself; knowledge of the school's programmes of study and processes; their child's targets; data on their child's progress; the next steps in their child's learning; and, the local community (in terms of wider opportunities, other support systems for parents and students; and community-based learning opportunities for both parent and student).

Leading parent engagement for achievement – 'yes, we can'

Successful PEPP school leaders make things happen and increase achievement by maximizing their leadership of parent engagement, by embedding the principles and practices of PEPP across the school, and by building on their existing strategies to improve school leadership at all levels. These school leaders also build professional relationships with other schools and the local community. This is achieved by school leaders by

- articulating a vision for the school that focuses on the achievement of all students;

- ensuring that teachers and other staff understand the role of the collection, analysis, and application of data to student progress and achievement and are able to act accordingly;

- ensuring that teachers and other staff are able to identify new, positive student behaviours and are able and supported to review and evaluate these;

- being good listeners in their interactions with staff and families;
- acknowledging the boundaries of their own professional knowledge and experience and valuing the professional input of others;
- including staff and other colleagues in strategic and student-level decision-making.

In addition, leadership of PEPP by school leaders involves appointing and supporting the school champion in terms of identifying students to participate in the programme, supporting the Welcoming Families and Collaborative Conversation modules, embedding PEPP in school planning/ school improvement plan, supporting provision of resources and supporting home–school visits.

Student progress in partnership with families

PEPP does not impose what or how schools should teach. Rather, PEPP encourages schools, with the support of the PEPP coach, to identify and evaluate what is already working well and build on that success. The Collaborative Conversations are designed to include the views of the student on their ambitions for achievement. For students to be able to do this effectively, it is vital that they and their parents have up-to-date feedback on the student's progress and achievements. This reliable data can then form the basis for setting agreed targets with parents and students in the Collaborative Conversations. When planning targets, schools consider how their current data systems allow them both to look back at students' previous attainment and build in high expectations of future attainment and progress.

Ambitious targets and challenge

The aim of PEPP is always for high-needs students to make accelerated progress, which is progress beyond what would be expected if they continued on their current trajectory. Ambitious targets for achievement and learning behaviours that are agreed in Collaborative Conversations need to reflect not only that current trajectory but also any additional challenge.

When setting targets, PEPP schools consider how their data systems allow for the following: the prior attainment of students to be used as the starting point for setting targets; targets that demonstrate high expectations of attainment and progress; and the current attainment trajectory of a student to be used as the basis for the setting of challenging targets that will accelerate the student's progress.

Students' targets in PEPP relate directly to the priorities identified by the parents in the Collaborative Conversation. They are written in a language that can be easily understood by the parents and the student. PEPP targets are based on something that the student will learn or a learning behaviour that they will improve.

Innovative approaches in partnership with students and families

In successful schools, innovative approaches are planned and agreed to by the parents and student; they are also time-specific, and carefully monitored. These can include many additional proven interventions that can add value to PEPP. The following section illustrates such an approach.

Seeing high-needs students in a new light

Good schools know that perhaps the most important thing for high-needs students is for them to be able to experience success at some level every day – whether that success is in reading, writing or maths at their own level, or in sports, performing arts or being a good friend. Engaging and understanding the views and experiences and ambitions of parents are key factors in recognizing and celebrating those successes. Within PEPP, teachers challenge attitudes towards high-needs students supported by informed discussions with families. For example, past attitudes towards people with disabilities generally, and towards people with learning challenges more particularly, can take a long time to change. PEPP schools often showcase the gifts of their high-needs students by small but significant actions, for example, engaging parents and families to celebrate the achievements of their children.

Families, schools and communities

PEPP schools have found that they can further enhance student achievement and progress by

- ensuring that students feel a sense of belonging to the school community.
- engaging with their local community and
- helping parents and students to engage with, and gain support from, the local community.

PEPP schools ensure that their high-quality teaching and learning draws upon resources available within the local community, and help parents to engage with opportunities and participate fully in their local community.

A sense of belonging

A sense of belonging to an overlapping series of communities is fundamental to the success of all students as they move through the school system. Most adults look back on their school days with nostalgia and affection because they felt they belonged to their home room, their class and their school and made often abiding friendships from early days. Facebook is testament to the affection that adults have for their schools – for the teachers who guided and cajoled them; for the special occasions – the school productions, the sporting triumphs and failures, the embarrassing photographs.

However, for many high-needs students such a sense of belonging simply does not exist. It does not exist because these students can feel that school has nothing to offer them – and does not care about them – and that they have nothing themselves to offer to their school. PEPP believes that all students have something to offer and that the effective school makes every student feel that they belong. PEPP supports schools to build on their already effective approaches and practice through tried and tested strategies for improving the attendance, behaviour, participation and overall well-being of high-needs students.

Communities in schools

One way to create a stronger sense of belonging for high-needs students is to effectively break down the boundaries of the school house. Particularly for older students, the challenge of the conventional, school-based learning setting is sometimes simply the wrong challenge. Seasoned educators will all recall high-needs students who have come alive through work experience, by helping with a community project or in an unconventional elective offered by a community volunteer. Yet other students find success in the very undercurrent of digital diversion and distraction that many schools see as a menace.

Community asset mapping

The concept and purpose of community asset mapping is based on developing a 'map' of community 'talents'. The opportunity provided by community asset mapping in the process of opening the school to a broader, richer learning curriculum is self-evident. In particular, this can be a very helpful way of extending the curriculum for reluctant or marginalized learners, and older students can be engaged in the mapping exercise itself.

Summary

Essentially, the leadership of parent engagement brings about real change and improves the aspirations, access and achievement of all students and their families. Schools face many obstacles to putting in place effective leadership for parent engagement, such as time, resources, and assumptions, (including assumptions about what parents are able and willing to contribute to their children's education). The PEPP framework is designed to support proven leaders to build on and maximize their leadership for parent engagement practices. In the next two sections, we examine (1) how the PEPP supports school leaders as change-makers in their leadership of parent engagement, and (2) the elements of the PEPP that will require strategic coordination from school leaders.

The following chapter provides a summary of the impact of PEPP based on evidence compiled by John Hopkins University.

PART SIX

Embedding the 3As – Aspiration, Access and Achievement

CHAPTER TWELVE

Evaluating the Impact of the Parent Engagement Partnership Program (PEPP)

I want to make sure our students and their parents feel respected and welcome here. I want them to be confident and learn what they need to and love coming to school.

I believe the teaching/learning process is a partnership between home and school. If this program will enhance that, I would like to be a part of it.

My professional practice goal this year was to increase parental involvement, so this program fits well with that goal.

(TEACHER REASONS FOR PARTICIPATING IN PEPP DURING
THE EARLY IMPLEMENTATION PHASE)

A key strength of the programme was teacher and head teacher motivation to participate in the PEPP programme and that is reflected in the above comments. In schools where the programme was implemented quickly, teachers were more confident about the programme and its potential impact on outcomes. This chapter considers findings from an independent evaluation of the baseline implementation (two to three months after starting) and case study analysis at the end of the Parent Engagement Partnership Program in the pilot schools in New York and carried out by John Hopkins University.

Context of the pilot in Massachusetts and New York

The pilot was carried out in three schools, representative of the educational phases. These included: an elementary school in Massachusetts (625 pupils in K–8); a middle school in Massachusetts (570 pupils in grades 6–8) and an academy in New York (over 800 students in grades 5–8).

Head teachers were enthusiastic about the programme at the outset and gave one or more of the following reasons for wanting to participate:

- current lack of parent engagement in the school
- a desire to focus on parent engagement
- a desire to support their teachers in developing parent engagement

In addition, one principal said that the teachers' request for a programme to address parent engagement and the principal finding out about PEPP 'came together at the same time'. Another principal said that the teachers were 'novices' in communication.

The external evaluators developed the evaluation process around the following questions; this chapter will consider findings from the final point:

- How is PEPP being used by teachers, school leaders, parents and students at each school with regard to programme-specific activities, home–school connections, teacher and parent communications, and school climate change?

- To what degree are major components of PEPP addressed at each school?
    - Welcoming Families
    - Collaborative Conversations
    - PEPP coach, school champion, and review team activities
    - Home–School Visits
    - Accelerated Learning Strategies
    - Community Assets Mapping

- What are the following major participants'/stakeholders' perceptions regarding the programme's value impacts on school climate and students' educational success?
    - teachers
    - parents

- ○ students
- ○ principals
- ○ PEPP coaches
- ○ school champions

- What are the trends in the following educational outcomes, particularly for the high-needs students?
  - ○ achievement
  - ○ attendance
  - ○ participation in extracurricular activities
  - ○ behaviour
- What are the strengths and weaknesses of the programme implementation, and recommendations for improvement?

A mixed-methods approach was employed by the evaluators to collect both quantitative and qualitative data from teachers, parents, school leaders and other key stakeholders. Data collection instruments included a teacher questionnaire distributed to teachers in the pilot schools (n = 30) and focusing on their early experiences of PEPP; and telephone interviews with the head teachers (n = 3), focusing on their reasons for becoming involved in PEPP, their hoped-for outcomes and their early experiences.

Results

Teacher knowledge of the programme prior to involvement and decisions to participate

Generally, teachers were not familiar with the programme prior to its implementation in the school. However, introductory presentations informed them of the goals of the programme: to increase engagement of parents in their child's education and schooling, to provide a platform for teachers to engage more meaningfully with parents and to sustain engagement. One teacher in a pilot school said:

> I was informed that it was a collaborative and impactful way to work with parents in the interest of the student.
> We were told it was an opportunity that we could take advantage of if we chose to do so.

Teachers generally had a personal interest in contributing to increased parental engagement and improving home–school partnerships. At the elementary school, teachers had highlighted this as an area for professional development. They were enthusiastic about developing their ideas and strategies for doing this; they were also keen to improve student outcomes, contributing to their student's future successes.

Professional development and support for implementing and continuing PEPP

Training for implementing and developing the programme in the schools varied in length, frequency and approach; as a result, the level of teachers' preparedness for implementing the PEPP programme varied. In schools where teachers had several training sessions, including a school-wide programme, they felt more prepared and 'somewhat confident' about implementing and developing the programme. This was particularly positive in the elementary school, where five meetings/training sessions had taken place. In addition, another strength of the programme was parents' enthusiasm for participating in the programme; early feedback from the elementary school indicated that 'parents have positive attitudes, loved the walkthrough and like having a voice'. Teachers in all schools were generally positive or very positive about the support from and interaction with the school champion. This is reflected in the following comments:

> the School Champion has been very helpful contacting parents and setting up meetings and gives great feedback ... they get to know parents' concerns, struggles, and reservations about school/child/classroom.
>
> (Teacher in Elementary school)

This has enabled one particular teacher to act on the information 'to reach out differently' than her 'previous methods of interaction'.

In another school, a teacher commented on the regular contact with the school champion about challenges with students:

> My PEPP School Champions are in contact with me regularly about the students we are working with. The support I receive is usually in school so that if we have issues with these students we work to resolve them and have in-school conversations.
>
> (Teacher at Academy)

Findings suggest that the school champion is important for the effective implementation and development of the programme in schools. Although teachers generally found the coach to be 'knowledgeable', 'understanding' and good at making 'recommendations', teachers had a stronger rapport with the school champion, who tended to provide the support and focus they needed for practice.

Parents' early reactions to the programme

The elementary school had involved parents more quickly at the outset than the middle school or the academy; parents were very enthusiastic about the programme. Although teachers at the three schools had not interacted directly with individual parents, the elementary school had conducted a walkthrough, which was very positive and is reflected in the following comments:

> I believe the parents that did a walkthrough of our school have a positive attitude towards building a relationship with their child's teachers and the school.
>
> I have not heard from the parents but those who did the visit left sticky notes with happy faces on classroom doors.
>
> I believe parents are very excited about being part of this whole process of the GEMS program that will help their child.

Head teacher and teacher perceptions of future impact of PEPP in their school

Overall, the training and implementation of the programme was most positive in the elementary school. This may have been due to the faster pace in implementing the programme, the higher number of training sessions, initial whole-school engagement, involvement of parents at the outset, and the enthusiasm of teachers to focus on this area as part of their continuing professional development.

In the elementary school, teachers were very positive about the future benefits of the programme. The majority were very or somewhat confident that their school would be inviting to families and conducive to learning. In addition, the majority of teachers believed that the programme would increase their skills to work more effectively with parents and students and positively impact on students' educational outcomes. In the other schools, teacher views were more varied, where the majority ranged from very or somewhat confident to unsure. However, feedback from staff to the head teacher was more positive, particularly in the middle school and the elementary school, where teachers found the programme to date 'very positive' or 'very good'. In the academy, the head teacher felt that staff believed the programme 'was still evolving, one step at a time'.

Looking to the future, head teachers viewed the programme within a staff development framework, where teachers were enabled to engage parents more fully in the learning and development of their children and through this improve children/student outcomes. This is reflected in the following head teacher comments:

> We want the parents to know that teachers are on the same page as them, not talking down to them.
> Right now it's limited to things like teacher conferences. There is no formal structure for involving parents.
> We would like to 'create parents as partners and ensure two-way communication'.
> The teachers are great about contacting parents if there is a problem, letting parents know about school events, etc., but it is one-way communication. Two-way communication between teachers and parents is currently not happening. We want communication with parents to be more than just a letter going home.
> We would like to 'use data for school change'.

Head teachers believed that the programme would help them to achieve their goals. Additionally, they would like more time, workshops, meetings, professional development and generally a faster pace in involving parents and students. Findings from the early implementation of PEPP have been generally positive, with teachers and head teachers feeling hopeful for positive outcomes from the development of the programme in their school. At the outset some teachers also had apprehensions about their confidence in realizing the goals in practice; however, as the above results reflect, these were unfounded.

Case studies

Sam made average progress in elementary school and made a successful and happy transfer to junior high. But, during his first year there, he has gradually begun to fall behind in English – it seems that he was not able to cope with lessons. At their first Collaborative Conversation, the teacher established that Sam's mother had great difficulties in learning to read and write in her native Urdu and that she had found it hard to learn English, despite living in the United States for over fifteen years. This information has prompted the teacher to suggest that Sam be tested for dyslexia (which Sam and his parents have agreed to), and to provide Sam's parents with information about English classes in the local community that could help them to support Sam's learning and learning behaviours.

In another school, a shy, withdrawn boy, Jack, takes much longer than his peers to produce any written work. He presses so heavily with his pencil that the physical process is hard work. The teacher and Jack's father agreed at the first Collaborative Conversation to encourage him each day to choose a word (a difficult word from his weekly words-to-learn list) and try to write the word as many times as possible, pressing as lightly as possible. Jack has called this his 'word races' and after only two weeks there has been definite improvement. The first Collaborative Conversation also revealed that Jack's counter-productive writing behaviour had developed in the previous year when he lost his mother to cancer. The teacher and Jack's father will use upcoming Collaborative Conversations to explore approaches to monitoring Jack's emotional well-being and how Jack could be provided with additional counselling and support.

Summary

Overall findings suggest that like Achievement for All, PEPP provides a possible path for developing teacher pedagogical skills and professional practice. Implemented at the school level and focusing on aspects of teaching/teacher quality, the programme will enable teacher development, without focusing on individual teacher performance.

The findings from this research were reported to the mayor's office at the Parent and Community Engagement Conference held in New York in October 2013. PEPP had been selected from an evaluation of eighty international parent and community engagement projects. Six projects participated in the conference, Achievement for All being the only European project. Recommendations from the conference were then developed for implementation by the incoming mayoral team. This acknowledgement was welcomed at the early stages of the national roll-out of the Achievement for All programme in England. This also supported further development of parent and carer engagement. The following chapter is focused more specifically on the 3As principles, which were applied to the development of middle leaders. The account is written by the author through a series of 'blogs' communicated during the delivery of a five-day programme in Seoul, South Korea.

CHAPTER THIRTEEN

South Korea: Development of Middle Leaders

Acclaimed for having one of the best education systems in the world and credited with transforming the country and growing the economy over the past sixty years, South Korea's success reflects a culture in which teachers and schools are highly respected. In 2011, Dwight School Seoul, a not for profit, international school was built with support from the Korean government; 30 per cent of the students are funded by the state. The school's mission statement is impressive: 'Dwight School Seoul is committed to finding and igniting the "spark of genius" in every child. Kindling their interests, we develop inquisitive, informed, self-aware, and ethical citizens who will build a better world.'

All spaces within the school are created for learning, focused on developing thinking skills, encouraging innovation and imparting knowledge. Following a recent international school inspection (CIS) visit report, the senior leadership team wanted to take the school to a 'higher' level, by training teachers to be leaders. The following case study sets out a successful middle leadership development programme at Dwight School. Focused on 'raising the bar', the case study is presented in the form of a diary written by the author, 31 August to 5 September 2015.

Day 1: Start of the academic year in Seoul

The start of the new academic year and I find myself at Dwight School in Seoul. I am leading a series of workshops for senior and middle leaders focused on inclusive leadership. They want to develop skills and understanding of a range of topics such as leadership style, managing others, team work, international management and professional development. After spending time supporting the senior leadership team, and explaining how the Achievement for All framework and 3As principles can benefit leaders, developing teams and individuals, while setting targets for the school, as well as individuals, there is full 'buy in' by the team – it seems that the world's best has an ambition to get even better!

The UK's education system has itself been greatly influenced by this vibrant, busy country I find myself in, with the school day, structure and teachers all very similar to that of our own, and the same emphasis on learning and outcomes as in the UK. With many countries facing the same challenges of raising standards within a context of inclusion hampered by financial constraints, it is self-evident that education systems around the world can learn more from one another.

Day 2: Culture, respect and investment

After spending half a day in the newly developed technology quarter in east Seoul, I find myself as a member of an elite, well-respected profession, that of teacher and professor. Education is a highly valued commodity in South Korea. It is also evident that government, business and communities place a significant investment in education. Why? It's a generational thing: grandparents and parents see their children as their future. Children and teenagers, in turn show deference and respect for their elders, including teachers.

The investment in the environment, buildings and appropriate learning spaces is self-evident; not an Arboretum or open staircase in sight! How is this so very different to the Building Schools for the Future investment? The answer is simple; all spaces are created for learning, with technology, books and open areas all focused on developing thinking skills, encouraging innovation; imparting knowledge and creativity in equal measure. The school is three years old; the building is inviting, encouraging and a calm safe place for children and young people to learn.

In classrooms that are so well equipped that IT is an integrated system – demonstrated by school announcements prepared, directed and delivered by the students from a purpose built studio – tablets are a must.

Culture, investment, ambition, value and respect are all words I have heard in relation to why education is such a high priority in Korea; results, higher education and employment follow.

Day 3: The challenge of assessment

I have enjoyed a fantastic day with middle and senior leaders at Dwight School Seoul. Their passion and enthusiasm for learning is evident, with all leaders demonstrating real commitment to improving inclusion through systems and pedagogy in their teams. 'Aiming high, moving the elevator to a higher level, engaging students in a ladder of success' are drivers that are to be adopted by the highly motivated and deeply engaged management team who have already started to plan how to put the theory from each of the workshop sessions into practice with their teams.

Framing the day with the Achievement for All four core elements: Leadership, Teaching and Learning, Parent and Carer engagement and wider outcomes and opportunities underpinned by 3As principles – Aspiration, Access and Achievement enabled me to demonstrate the programme and its impact in around 4,000 schools, currently engaging 172,111 students in England and Wales. In a similar fashion to Achievement for All, Dwight School Seoul has a target group comprising their lowest learners (10 per cent of the school). Known as the Quest group these children make significantly greater progress than their peers. Why? Because of individualized learning and the dedicated team of teachers tasked with improving their learning. The challenge for the middle leaders is how to adapt this practice to the whole school; this is where the Achievement for All framework and 3As principles will help, by providing a framework for practice.

Learning and thinking together is facilitating the development and growth of strategic plans at school and department levels. They are also building a response to a recent inspection report, entitled 'Good to Great', by focusing on the developmental relationship between leaders, teachers, parents and carers and students.

A big practical consideration is assessment. As with the national curriculum in England, the International Baccalaureate has undergone significant changes in recent years. Dwight School Seoul has invested a great deal in developing an exciting and challenging curriculum, which is assessed on an individual student and class level; this needs to move to a common framework for the whole school to enable further analysis to support higher standards and impact on pedagogy.

Day 4: Internationalization and internationalism

A discussion on internationalization and internationalism was revealing in that the school had just introduced an instruction to students to only speak English during the school day so that all students would feel included in every conversation. The school has a fairly healthy intake of nationalities from America, Europe, Asia and Australasia; staff are largely British, Canadian and Australian, joining American, South African and Dutch colleagues.

Opportunities for the students are many, ranging from Varsity sports leagues to field trips and the inevitable university recruitment fairs. A developing provision for English as an Additional Language (EAL) and Special Educational Needs (SEN) ensures that all students' needs will be identified and development supported.

The middle and senior management workshops had taken the schools leaders to the next step. This was to be the 'dawn of a new day' for the staff. New levels of accountability, whole school development and sharing of practice were to 'ignite the spark of genius' in the leaders. The response was fantastic. Immersed in the need to adopt a cross-school system for recording student progress and outcomes, each leader contributed ideas that led to the basis of a framework for combining the assessment of three to eighteen-year-olds being developed in an afternoon. Amazing!

Day 5: Engaging parents and carers

My presentation in the Dwight School Seoul Lecture Theatre was on the importance of partnering and valuing parents in improving outcomes for all. Dwight senior and middle leaders were in agreement, the questions were flowing – What about the capacity and skills of staff to commit the time? What happens with older teenagers? What about the time in the school year? How does this work with high-achieving students?

During the week teachers had been challenged by high net worth parents wanting more for their children – the Achievement for All 'structured conversation' could provide the framework needed, giving order to the communication, needs and wants of parents. The pressure of Korean ambition weighs heavily on the shoulders of the leaders at Dwight School. There is scope for development; there is also scope for development of Achievement for All in partnership with Korean leaders.

We move from the formality of the Lecture Theatre upstairs back to the Gallery, a large open space containing the exhibits produced by Dwight students from New York, Toronto, Sang Hai, London and Seoul. Aspirational and reflective pieces demonstrated the skill of the artists, their anxieties and ambitions for their personal futures. Dwight leaders were challenged to consider their own futures and how this played out in relation to the school and students. The level of inspirational thought was as inspiring as the pictures and sculptures around us. Reflections on their career journeys, and their shared desire to improve and open up the possibilities for all students, were humbling.

What next?

Working in an international school is as pressured as any environment – there is a sense of commitment, vocation and awareness – and unique to the shared endeavour and the potential sense of isolation created by the distance from home. These are the education adventurers, ready to tackle all that the mysteries of travel, culture and the International Baccalaureate throw at them. I am in awe of them, their families and the standard of education they deliver.

Wanting more for their students and staff we moved to the here and now, as is inevitable in any workshop – what was going to happen next? How to take their evolving ideas as senior and middle leaders to the next stage?

We considered motivation, strategic and operational goals, evaluation and outcomes. My new colleagues were up for the task, focused, methodical, supportive and ready to turn the next corner in their exciting journey.

The day ended in the gym, where we sat alongside the school volleyball teams, supporting each other in their pre Varsity league matches, a warm up for the matches to come. The commitment, skill and understanding of the players, reflecting a desire to improve, provided a parallel to the middle leadership programme.

Middle leaders are player managers, they look to their leaders, play their part as members of their teams, pupils and parents, and that of the middle leadership team; they represent their school and they aim for their team to win.

Summary

Engaging with teachers as they developed their understanding of middle leadership for inclusion was illuminating. The challenges set by the senior leadership team were well received, with a shared commitment to improve outcomes for all students. Policy (at school level) mirrored practice.

From a personal perspective I felt privileged to have been invited to lead this programme. It was the first time in my (long) career where I felt that all teachers were respected for their knowledge, skills and commitment to learning. The teachers were enthusiastic and engaged in their classrooms and around the school environs. There was a significant sense of 'can do', their aspirations were based on high expectations for all pupils.

There are a number of challenges that were readily acknowledged by the teachers, assessment and special educational needs featured in every session. These issues will have been raised by the new middle tier for discussion with the senior team, I will remain in contact with the staff to follow their journey into leadership in Seoul and across the international school arena.

The following chapters consider the possible implications of the international perspectives described in this book on policy and practice at national government, and local school levels. Each provides evidence-informed recommendations for policy, system and school leaders that will result in improving the progress of all children and young people, particularly those identified with SEN or disability.

PART SEVEN
Policy and Practice

CHAPTER FOURTEEN

Bringing SEND into the Classroom: Implications for Policy

In recent years there has been a drive across Organization for Economic Co-operation and Development (OECD) countries and economies to close the achievement gap for children and young people with SEND and others at risk of underperformance. Although advances have been made in some education systems, with some success, those which have employed a whole school, collaborative framework incorporating teaching and learning, leadership, and parental/carer engagement have been able to do it better. This chapter focuses on policy recommendations at a national government and local school levels.

Policy recommendation 1: The 3As principles – Aspiration, Access and Achievement

While an aspirational vision has characterized education policy across some countries in recent years, it has not always been borne out in the school system. Recent research, across OECD countries showed that over the last decade many countries have made little progress in helping their weakest students improve their performance in reading, mathematics and science (OECD, 2016). What is clear, however, is the need for a stronger focus across all countries on aspiration. Findings from one of the largest studies of a programme for children and young people with SEND in Europe involving 28,000 pupils, highlighted the better outcomes of pupils when there is a culture of high aspirations (Humphrey and Squires, 2011); development of an aspirational culture was coupled with focused teacher professional development.

Menzies (2013) suggests that low attainment may blunt the aspirational vision of disadvantaged pupils. Whatever the reason, the message is clear. Quality teaching needs to be accompanied by the development of an aspirational outlook and the opportunity for its realization.

The research studies described in this book have illustrated the impact of the Achievement for All programme and 3As principles in schools in England, Wales, Norway, Lithuania, and the potential impact in Latvia and South Korea. But how is this best achieved? Is it enough to focus on teachers and teaching? Or do we need a whole-school approach? Focusing on teaching alone may not be enough; there needs to be a focused whole-school collaborative approach to the development of an aspirational outlook; in essence a whole-school cultural shift to ensure that every child has the opportunity to fulfil their potential. Unleashing aspiration across schools may provide the impetus for change, but it is most effective when it is channelled through a framework. This chapter proposes an evidence-informed policy framework across the key areas of leadership, teaching and learning, parent and carer engagement and wider outcomes for education systems across the world.

Policy Recommendation 2: The Achievement for All framework

Element 1: Leadership

Bringing SEND into the classroom is dependent on effective inclusive leadership, supported by the Achievement for All framework, and founded on

- a strong **vision** for ALL pupils, supported in equal measures by **commitment, collaboration and effective communication** with parents, pupils, teachers and leaders.

- **strong values** demonstrated by the behaviour of staff, governors and pupils.

- **leadership strategies,** embedding Achievement for All in all classrooms.

- **professional development** for all leaders, teachers and support practitioners to engage pupils and parents in learning.

Leading learning in a positive way is founded on aspiration, access and achievement being applied to all learners. In order for pupils to become aspirational in the school environment or to continue to raise their aspirations, it is crucial for staff to be aspirational for them. Without a whole-school culture which models aspirational values and holds a strong belief in the pupils' abilities to access and achieve, it is difficult for them to do so.

School leadership: Developing ethos and culture

School leaders, teachers and support teachers have a profound impact on all children and young people by raising their aspirations and achievements and improving their access to learning. A measure of a school's effectiveness is the ability of the staff to work as an organization towards achieving the school's vision underpinned by a shared set of values and beliefs. School leaders have a distinctive role in initiating this approach, which contributes to the development of ethos and culture across the school.

Donnelly (2000: 135–6), by offering two definitions, which 'reflect either a positivist or anti-positivist view', highlights the difficulty in delineating ethos. A positivist would view ethos, she suggests, as 'a formal expression of the authorities' aims and objectives for an organisation'. Anti-positivists, on the other hand, 'see ethos as something which is more informal emerging from social interaction and process' (Donnelly, 2000: 150). The resultant reality in the learning community she suggests is that 'ethos is not a static phenomenon but rather … a "negotiated" process whereby individuals come to some agreement about what should and should not be prioritised'.

Schools leaders influence the development of ethos by shaping the processes and practices which develop across the school. Differences between schools, related to the age of the children and community context, may be explained in terms of organizational and social structure, which are also reflected in the interpersonal relationships of those within the school (e.g. adult–child interactions, adult–adult interactions and child–child interactions). These factors, which permeate the school to such an extent that they drive it towards achieving goals, contribute to the development of an ethos.

Together, the three elements of organizational and social structure and interpersonal relationships, affect the culture of the setting, and are, in turn, influenced by it. Peters and Waterman (2004: 75), in their book *In Search of Excellence*, highlight the 'dominance and coherence of culture' in strongly performing companies, where all employees share a common set of values. Figure 14.1 clearly shows how the three elements of social environment, policy, systems and structures and actions and behaviours are linked.

The relationship between the elements in Figure 14.1 determines the degree of consonance operating in the school. Where there is dissonance, or disharmony, between these elements, energy gets diverted away from the central educational task (e.g. it might be expended on such activities as mediating conflict or counteracting the consequences of suppressed resentment). But where there is a high degree of consonance, or consistency,

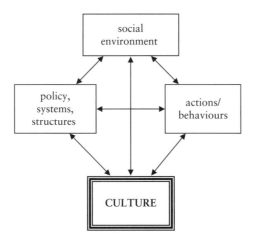

FIGURE 14.1 *Factors influencing setting culture*
Source: Blandford and Shaw, 2001: 54

the school's values are more recognizable, and the school is likely to provide an agreeable and productive atmosphere for learning. The high degree of consonance between the three factors influencing culture is manifested in the practices.

Element 2: Teaching and learning

Teaching: The whole-school approach

In England, Sutton Trust research (2011) highlighted the quality of teaching as the biggest single factor in the achievement of children; the report considered it particularly critical for those from disadvantaged backgrounds. In practice, however, quality teaching is not easily defined (Coe et al., 2014). In their recent review of great teaching they highlighted the difficulties in defining it outside a quantitative framework. Evidence showed that it is most frequently delineated within the context of student achievement; they defined it as that 'that which leads to improved student progress'. The definition perhaps shows the difficulties for practice and is summed up by the American poet of the last century:

> There are two kinds of teachers: the kind that fill you with so much quail shot that you can't move, and the kind that just gives you a little prod behind and you jump to the skies.
>
> (Robert Frost)

Undoubtedly, every school would aspire to have the inspirational teacher described by Frost. In practice, this may call for a whole-school cultural shift to ensure that no child is left behind. The Sutton Trust (2011) research showed that poor children can gain as much as 1.5 years of learning with a very effective teacher, in comparison to 0.5 years with a less effective teacher. Often governments respond to poor teaching by focusing on teacher development and improved initial teacher education. This, however, only addresses part of the problem; it needs to be coupled with the development of a whole-school values-driven way of working.

In a values-driven system, the needs of each pupil – those with SEND and others vulnerable to underachievement – can be the focus of every teacher, every lesson, every day. Improving 'just' teacher quality or 'just' leadership is not enough. There needs to be a synergy across key areas and systems – leadership, teaching and learning, parental engagement and wider outcomes.

There needs to be a deeper understanding of achievement which does not focus on teaching alone but also on the development in learners of an aspirational outlook. This is particularly relevant for children and young people with SEND and others who are vulnerable to underperformance. Evidence from the OECD showed the better performance of students in countries where 'teachers, parents and citizens' believed all students could reach high standards (OECD, 2010). The report highlighted the more 'equitable distribution of learning outcomes' where 'teachers and schools' embraced 'diverse student populations through personalised educational pathways'. The case for a more inclusive approach to education is reaffirmed by Barber et al. (2012: 54):

> You can't tell where the great ideas are going to come from, so it is essential to unlock the talents of everyone. ... In short, education systems today need to get everyone onto a platform of high minimum standards. To put it differently, they must place a high floor under every student's feet.

Teacher beliefs, values and attitudes

A strong, values-driven school culture can militate against the impact of teacher beliefs, attitudes and values, which differ from those of the school. Values can be thought of as the assumptions inherent in the culture. They define the norms by which people of the same culture live and will be expressed in actions. They are often viewed within an ethical context; where for an individual, they may have an absolute value. In schools, they can be taken for granted and will not be overtly articulated. However, unless they are articulated, teacher values which are contrary to school values can undermine the ethos and culture which is developed.

In the day-to-day life within settings, culture affects the manner in which all members of the community relate to each other. Culture which develops in a school may be visible and explicit, or vague and implicit. It may be strong and dominant, or virtually impotent. A helpful culture might be defined as the way in which all of us in this workplace agree to work together in order to provide the best service for the learners. On the surface, this provides a simple framework, but the question of operationalizing cultures (attitudes to other staff, children and parents and the values which are developed) can be difficult in practice. In the context of children's learning and development this is highly significant. An effective school will have considered values as a collaborative exercise: What is our vision? What is our mission? What do we stand for? And how will this be manifested in practice?

In attempting to analyse education culture further, the elements which affect it could be categorized into the following three groups:

The social environment, that is, the background against which the school processes take place. This includes the cultures represented, the gender balance, the maturity and experience of staff, the geographical position, the physical nature of the buildings and the nature of the community from which the school draws its intake. It has an underlying effect on the way people work, affecting the community's expectations of each other and consequently impacts on the extent to which the aims are achieved.

The formal management systems, policies and structures. Implicit and unintentional messages may be conveyed by the answers to questions such as:

- To what extent do the support and learning systems cohere? (e.g. does staff training and development support children's learning and outcomes?) – to what extent does the educational (as opposed to the profit) agenda drive decisions?
- Are staff encouraged to develop 'on-the-job', or are teachers treated as expendable items that must be replaced with a model that is already trained for the latest development.

The actions and behaviours of the people in the school. These determine ultimately how policy is implemented. This area is hard to legislate for because it depends on willingness and ability, which is closely linked with attitude and skills. As people are inevitably influenced by, and respond to, the way they themselves are treated, the responsibility of the school leader to set an example and create a conducive atmosphere.

There is research which indicates that developing a distinctive organizational culture is a powerful tool in helping people to work together regardless of their own cultural programming (e.g. Kanter and Corn, 1994; Cray and Mallory, 1998). Experience in many educational settings has shown that those which have consciously focused on developing their own distinctive culture, starting with agreed values and bringing together the policies, systems, structures, and behaviours of the school into a state of consonance, create communities of practice where children can achieve their full potential. For this to be effective teachers and other staff need to be aware of how their ideas, attitudes, values and beliefs can and do influence what happens in practice (e.g. the way they question children to encourage thinking and learning).

The idea that teacher professional development had a strong social dimension was given force in the late 1990s by Etienne Wenger (1998). In proposing the term 'community of practice' to describe learning within an organization, he provided a theoretical base for the learning process. He argued that all learning has a social dimension and through interaction, learning takes place. Effective knowledge transfer through social participation cannot overlook the ethos and culture of the educational organization.

Element 3: Parent and carer engagement

As the research in England, Wales, Norway and the United States has illustrated, a key factor in the development of a school 'learning' community is the extent to which parents and carers are engaged in their children's learning. Parent and carer engagement in children's learning has a very distinct and far-reaching effect on their outcomes. Research across OECD countries and economies showed the greater confidence and motivation of children whose parents had high expectations for their learning and achievement (Schleicher, 2014).

Parent and carer engagement in children's learning is about schools and teachers working in partnership with parents. It is about schools giving parents the opportunity to talk about their child, their aspirations for their learning, their strengths and what they enjoy. It is also about teachers learning from parents, jointly setting learning targets with parents and ensuring this informs classroom planning. Schools which are particularly effective in engaging parents and carers as partners in their child's learning have seen improved attainment and accelerated progress in children's outcomes (PwC, 2014; Humphrey and Squires, 2011).

Element 4: Wider opportunities and wider outcomes

Research shows that when children engage in wider activities they have higher academic achievement (Catterall, 2012; Metsapelto and Pulkkinen, 2012; Ofsted, 2008) and improved well-being (Ofsted, 2008). Regrettably, for children with SEND, they often do not access the wider provision; this is equally true for other vulnerable groups (Looked After Children and those from socio-economic disadvantage). Evidence from the Achievement for All pilot in England (DfE, 2011) showed that children and young people with SEND were less likely to access extracurricular opportunities provided by schools than their peers (Humphrey and Squires, 2011). This is also supported by the wider literature; in the United States, Carter (2010) highlights the opportunities missed by high-school students with disabilities (this includes building relationships with peers and developing leadership skills) because they do not access the wider provision.

Much of the existing research literature in the field of wider or extracurricular activities comes from international studies, particularly from the United States and is focused on high-school (secondary level) pupils. Recent studies highlight the positive benefits to children and young people's achievement when they engage in extracurricular activities. Catterall (2012) explored the benefits for 'at risk' youth of engaging in arts programmes in the United States. Using data from four large national, longitudinal databases, the researchers found that disadvantaged children and young people who engaged both with arts programmes and learning reached levels of academic achievement closer to or greater than the national population studied.

Knifsend and Graham (2012), also in the United States, using a sample of 864 multi-ethnic, high-school pupils (eleventh and twelfth grade) explored the impact of participation in extracurricular activities on pupil sense of belonging at school and academic engagement and achievement. They also considered the extent (number of activities) and length (time spent) of involvement across four areas: academic/leadership groups, arts activities, other clubs and sports. Their findings showed that when students were involved in two areas only they had a stronger sense of belonging at school and higher achievement on point scores in eleventh grade and better academic engagement in twelfth grade. Involvement in more than two activities showed a non-linear relationship, suggesting that involvement in too many extracurricular activities may have a negative impact on student outcomes.

Findings from research carried out by Fredericks (2012), which also considered the breadth and intensity of extracurricular activities in which students participated, showed the general falling off in academic achievement when students were involved in more activities. On average, the researcher found that tenth-grade students participated in two to three hours of extracurricular activities for five hours per week. Using data from the Educational Longitudinal Study of American high-school students (sample size: 13,130), Fredericks found that when tenth-grade students (fifteen years old) had moderate engagement with extracurricular activities, there was a positive association with maths test scores and grades and raised educational expectations at twelfth grade (seventeen years old). However, her findings showed that when students did more activities for longer periods of time there was a decrease in 'academic adjustment'.

In Finland, a three-year longitudinal study with a relatively moderate sample of 281 children aged nine to ten explored the impact of participation in extracurricular activities on children's socio-emotional behaviour and academic achievement (Metsapelto and Pulkkinen, 2012). Findings showed that, when children participated in arts, crafts and music activities, they had better attainment in maths, reading and writing. They also had greater concentration, perseverance and took more care over their work (working skills); when children participated in extracurricular drama they also had better working skills. Findings further showed that when children participated in academic clubs, they were less likely to internalize problems and their academic performance improved. Recent data analysis of student participation in extracurricular science across OECD countries and economies also highlights better academic performance (OECD, 2012). Findings also showed that in most countries, where students participated in extracurricular science activities, they had a stronger self-belief in their ability to do science and had greater enjoyment of the subject.

The development of a broad extracurricular programme, alongside the main curriculum, has yet to be realized across schools across countries. Provision in some nation-state education systems and some schools within countries is excellent, with appropriate activities, implemented and developed through contribution from the pupil 'voice' and designed to complement pupil learning in the main curriculum; regrettably, this type of provision is piece meal.

A recent study in England by the Early Intervention Foundation found that of all social and emotional skills developed in childhood, self-control and self-regulation matter most consistently for how children fare when they become adults. For example, better self-control is strongly associated with mental well-being; good physical health and in getting a job and increasing income (Goodman et al., 2015). In schools where pupils are provided with opportunities outside of the main curriculum, pupil academic and wider outcomes have been good (Humphrey and Squires, 2011; PwC, 2014). There is scope for all schools to increase their wider provision for children, further developing opportunities for better outcomes and success.

Creating and implementing a good inclusion policy

The inclusion policy will be set within the context of the school's vision, mission and aims set out in the school improvement plan (SIP). Figure 14.2 illustrates the relationship between vision, mission and aims, where the central core represents the vision, the second circle represents the aims of the school and the outer circle represents the mission.

The inclusion policy will relate clearly to the school's vision and be central to school leadership by involving all teachers in the process of identifying its aims and objectives. The implementation plan should identify, along with other school initiatives, curriculum and assessment. All policies need also to reflect school, local and national government policies. The main purpose of any plan should be to improve the quality of teaching and learning for all pupils.

More broadly, leaders need to consider how those vulnerable to underachievement contribute to the development of a learning environment for a community of learners. A fundamental element of learning and teaching

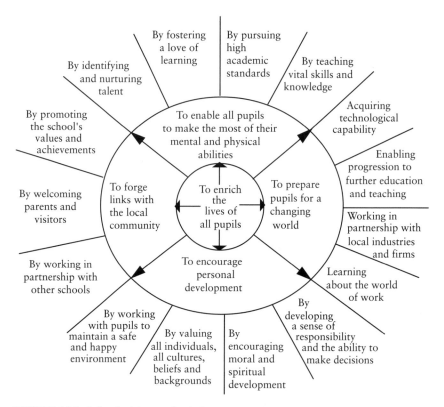

FIGURE 14.2 *School vision and mission statements*

is the self-esteem of pupils, teachers and the senior leadership team. Without self-esteem, pupils and teachers will not function in the school community. There is a need for every school to have an inclusion policy that focuses on personal development and growth. Busher (2000: 52) underlines the importance of 'creating an inclusive school, of developing staff abilities to improve the quality of learning opportunities students have'. An inclusion policy should reflect the ethos of the school and contribute to the fulfilment of its mission.

As with SIPs, an inclusion policy will reflect the values and beliefs of the school community. It should also relate to the social development of pupils as appropriate to their age and personal needs. Each school will need to have a view on what they particularly wish to encourage; but all schools will need to foster the development of desirable attitudes and personal qualities which can relate to the knowledge and understanding, skills and abilities of the members of their community.

Schools complement and extend the functions of the home and wider community by helping to prepare all pupils to live in society. Pupils need to learn the obligations that go with membership of a group and a community.

The development of personal values is an outcome of an effective inclusion policy that relates to the social function of each school and academy. Pupils also need to become aware of their own identity as individuals and of the importance of taking account of the feelings and wishes of others.

In practice, teachers provide a range of opportunities for pupils to learn and develop social skills and attitudes. The process of social development is continued throughout primary and secondary education, in school rules and codes of practice, in school councils and clubs and in the encouragement of pupils' responsibility for themselves and others.

Teachers will benefit from a clear and agreed inclusion policy that has expectations of them as practitioners. Effective teachers operating under clearly understood guidelines feel confident when giving instructions and are able to develop targets for pupils and teachers.

The school community must determine the precise content of an inclusion policy. There is a huge difference between simply having an inclusion policy on paper and having one that actually works well in practice. In practice, an inclusion policy will be a comprehensive and assertive statement intended to guide the school community (Blandford and Knowles, 2013). The policy will be the outcome of a democratic decision-making process involving all members of the school community; participation is the key to an effective policy.

Summary

As this chapter has shown, social and economic background has little to do with underperformance. Against a background of low aspirations, poor access to learning and an uninviting future for those who leave school without basic literacy and numeracy, the particular framework outlined in this chapter has shown outcomes beyond expectations when aspiration, access and achievement are applied to all learners. This framework is Achievement for All underpinned by the 3As principles.

The recent OECD report (2016) – 'Low performing students – why they fall behind and how to help them succeed' highlighted the importance of government's implementing the 'right policies' to address low performance. The report called for a change in approach to 'break the cycle of disengagement and low performance'. These included: identifying low performers and designing a tailored policy strategy; reducing inequalities in access to early education; providing remedial support as early as possible; encouraging the involvement of parents and local communities; providing targeted support to disadvantaged schools or families and offering special programmes for immigrant, minority-language and rural students (OECD, 2016); this is similar to the Achievement for All approach.

The Achievement for All programme, delivered in partnership by school leaders, teachers, parents and carers, pupils and support professionals is wholly focused on improving the aspirations, access and achievement of all pupils. The shift in head teacher and teacher attitude to teaching and learning and their development of more inclusive practices through the Achievement for All framework – as a result of a greater focus on identification of those vulnerable to low performance – supports and encourages raised teacher aspirations and expectations for all children.

Achievement for All, 'which have been successful in raising the ambitions and achievement of pupils with SEND' (Ofsted, 2013: 60) – demonstrated in England and also in Wales, the United States, Norway, Latvia, Lithuania and South Korea – can provide an effective framework for supporting and driving improvement in schools across other nation states. Its effectiveness is perhaps best summed up by head teachers of schools in the Achievement for All pilot who cited the following 'inclusive leadership' lessons learnt from their leadership of Achievement for All in their schools.

- 'Our culture of engagement and aspiration has improved, and so lessons are more focused and behaviour is better, which also benefits other pupils.'

- 'Achievement for All has helped us focus on aspirational outcomes. Planning for SEND children is now more parent- and pupil-centred.'

- 'The whole school has benefitted from Achievement for All. We are seeing excellent progress in all children, along with more effective teaching and learning practices.'

Ultimately, it will be the leaders who will decide on policies, it is hoped that they will have courage and be a risk taker ('change and bend the rules to match your own context'). By which the recommendation would be to focus on the creation of SEND policies advised by this research and to use what has been learnt for children with SEND to focus on wider groups of children within the school.

At the national – government, and local – school levels, it is the intention that the reader will be committed to the progress of **all** children and young people.

The following chapter describes how this might be achieved, concluding this book with a focus on evidence-informed practice.

CHAPTER FIFTEEN

Bringing SEND into the Classroom: Implications for Practice

Bringing SEND into the classroom through the Achievement for All 3As approach is about developing a system where every child is valued. SEND can be perceived as a specialist area, not for the many but the few. However, if every child is provided with the opportunity to achieve regardless of their background, challenge or need, then SEND is and should be the concern of all school leaders and teachers. This means being ready and well equipped to give your best for those children who might be at risk of underachievement. In practice it means providing the right sort of support to ensure that children achieve, are confident, develop an ability to communicate their own views and make successful transitions through their education – early years to school, school to adulthood. Parents and carers should be 'active' participants in the process. This chapter will consider how a system, valuing every child, is achieved in practice – the issues and implications – and will offer possible solutions to the challenges which can face leaders and teachers in developing and sustaining an inclusive school.

SEND practice: Founded on inclusive policies

In England, the SEND Code of Practice 0-25 (DfE/DoH, 2014) set out the statutory guidance for practice. For all those working with children and young people with SEND and their families, the following principles should underpin practice:

- Take into account the views of children, young people and their families.

- Enable children, young people and their parents to participate in decision-making.

- Collaborate with partners in education, health and social care to provide support.

- Identify the needs of children and young people.

- Make high-quality provision to meet the needs of children and young people.

- Focus on inclusive practices and removing barriers to learning.

- Help children and young people to prepare for adulthood.

(*Source*: Adapted from DfE, 2014: 5)

These principles are as applicable in other countries as they are in England. As school educators, teachers and leaders, focus on SEND principles, there needs to be an awareness of their positive impact on the whole community in day-to-day practice. What are its values? What are the current tensions? What do you hope to achieve for children in your care? How can it be done in an inclusive way, that is, working both in and with the community? In order to answer these questions teachers must locate themselves as individuals within the community, becoming aware of their specific roles in helping the community to function inclusively and successfully.

Leading change within the classroom

High-quality teaching and learning enables teachers, leaders and other educationalists to improve the attainment and progress of all pupils. It is based on teachers, pupils and their parents knowing where the children are in their learning, where they are aiming to get and how to get there. It is founded on collaborative working and active learning. But what does it 'look' like in practice?

For schools it means

- strong whole-school assessment systems in place.

- having good policies for marking and feedback.

- good monitoring and evaluation approaches to processes and practices.

For teachers it means

- knowing your pupils and how they learn.

- having high aspirations for their learning.

- giving children a sense of ownership of learning.

- taking a more personalized approach to children's learning.

- keeping good records.

For pupils it means

- being able to access the curriculum.

- having teachers who raise their aspirations and increase their achievements.

- having confidence in their own capabilities.

- having high self-esteem.

- having self-mastery skills.

For parents it means

- knowing where their child is in their learning.

- knowing how to support them in their learning.

- having high aspirations for their learning and achievement.

(*Source*: Blandford and Knowles, 2013)

As illustrated in this book, the implementation and development of high-quality teaching and learning is centred on the key areas of effective engagement of children and parents and carers, assessment, data tracking, measurement of progress, target setting, suitable teaching approaches (high-quality teaching), appropriate interventions and staff with a good knowledge and understanding of how all children learn and achieve. It is founded on high aspirations for pupil outcomes developed across the school. In essence, when there is a rigorous, high-quality approach to these areas, the attainment and progress of children and young learners is significantly improved.

It is often not what schools state what they do – schools frequently cite similar areas of focus for improvement – but the particular systems that are in place, the particular approach and the depth to which it is carried out. The Education Endowment Foundation commissioned Durham University team of researchers to analyse common elements of quality teaching suggested by evidence they list six:

- content knowledge (pedagogical)
- quality of instruction and classroom climate
- classroom management
- teacher beliefs and
- professional behaviour.

(*Source*: Coe et al., 2014: 3–4)

In practice, these are borne out differently in the classroom and across the school. Quality teaching can help pupils surmount generation-long barriers to learning, but the particular approaches and strategies need to be well embedded into the regular practice and culture of the school. In addressing the six elements of quality teaching outlined by Coe at al. (2014), the synergy between the elements is a key consideration.

The Achievement for All pilot also investigated these areas: Teacher beliefs – the reasons why they adopt particular practices and their theories about learning – can be a central area for reflection. By changing levels of aspiration held by pupils, teachers and parents and carers, pupils become more motivated and teachers begin to adapt their established beliefs and behaviours raising their expectations; the result is improved pupil progress (Humphrey and Squires, 2011). Encouraging teachers to develop themselves, deepening their subject knowledge and learning to use it as effectively as possible is self-evident. What can be lacking is a focus on the synergy between the other elements of quality teaching and the extent to which models of distributed leadership are effectively developed across the school; the latter enables teachers to 'take ownership' for change.

Teachers' sense or 'feeling' of responsibility for the learning and achievement of pupils in their class can be the axis on which quality of instruction turns. Improving content knowledge needs to be coupled with improvement in instruction based on: careful assessment and analysis of pupil data, effective target setting (which help pupils to improve) and the engagement of parents and carers in the learning process. Research evidence shows that when teachers are given responsibility for the pupils in their classroom, supported by senior leaders and provided with focused training, pupil academic and wider outcomes are significantly improved.

Such positive teacher practices include:

- taking a more active role in the assessment and monitoring of pupils;
- being more frequently involved in reviewing individual pupil targets;

- having data-led discussions with the senior leadership team (SLT) – providing opportunity to identify pupils not making the expected progress and finding appropriate interventions to help them;

- planning with other teachers for differentiation – allowing for greater focus on individual pupils;

- employing the 'structured conversation' model with parents of identified children – enabling teachers to change their own and parent's expectations of pupils and recognizing their potential (this framework for developing focused discussion between the teacher, parent and their child is employed in the *Achievement for All* programme);

- seeing how increased teacher knowledge and understanding of pupils results in a more personalized approach to teaching and learning within the classroom and seeing continuing professional development (CPD) and other training opportunities as helpful.

(*Source*: Humphrey and Squires, 2011)

Professional behaviours linked to professional development are most effective when they include not only the development of teacher skills, but those of parents and carers. Parents are enabled to become 'real' partners in their child's education, contributing to accelerated progress. High standards of behaviour are achieved across classrooms when pupils feel valued and want to belong to their school. The quality of interaction between teachers and students as well as teacher expectation is enhanced by addressing effective communication and interaction skills across the curriculum. In helping children to develop as independent and confident learners, head teachers, teachers and other staff need to give particular attention to the creation of a positive environment. A stimulating learning environment will produce stimulating results. These elements identified by Coe and his colleagues, which have just been introduced in overview, will now be explored in some greater detail.

Teaching approaches: Avoiding 'forever failures'

In contrast to Achievement for All, Coe et al. (2014) were critical of praising children as a means of encouraging learning and progress. They suggested that it may inhibit further development by inadvertently giving out the message that 'this is the best you can ever be'. However, appropriate feedback and praise for those vulnerable to underachievement is vital; teachers need to avoid putting them into a situation where they become the 'forever failures'.

For those with low attainment, learning should be broken down into small sections and appropriate feedback provided; children need to develop self-confidence and confidence in their competencies. This involves 'enabling' an internal change in the child, supporting and encouraging them to develop a positive disposition to learning and achievement. Effective approaches include:

- making learning relevant and helping pupils understand the purpose of their learning;

- teachers refining their teaching strategies – especially questioning skills and other ways to engage every pupil in the class;

- ensuring curriculum is relevant to all pupils – in many cases this may involve adjusting and reshaping the curriculum and the way it is presented and making sure that pupils see mistakes as valuable learning lessons.

Children being aware of their own learning gaps and needs is a key step in the learning journey, but it is important that no pupil is set up to fail.

Learning to be an inclusive school

Achievement for All is not something that can be made to happen from outside a school or even by the commitment of a few dedicated individuals from the school staff. Achievement for All requires ownership by the head teacher and senior leadership team, governors and all staff (NCSL, 2011). It also requires willingness on the part of schools to analyse their own practice and to identify areas where they could improve. This chapter will consider the importance of leadership across the school in implementing and developing the Achievement for All framework; the place of monitoring and evaluation for effective and improving practice is explored.

Over recent years, the UK government education policy reflects the increasing influence of international research relating to 'high performing' and 'improving' education systems and the place of school leaders and teachers. The 2007 McKinsey report – 'How the world's best performing school systems come out on top' – highlighted the central role of teachers in improving children's outcomes:

> The quality of an education system cannot exceed the quality of its teachers; the only way to improve outcomes is to improve instruction; and achieving universally high outcomes is only possible by putting in place mechanisms to ensure that schools deliver high quality instruction to every child.

> (Barber and Mourshead, 2007: 43)

The follow-up report in 2010 – 'How the World's Most Improved School Systems Keep Getting Better', (Mourshead, Chijioke and Barber, 2010) showed the central role of head teachers in leading improvement and managing change.

Providing opportunities for every child, changing cultures and increasing expectations is realized in schools through the engagement of senior leaders. The particular Achievement for All model acknowledges the current emphasis on systems leadership (Fullan, 2004) as an effective approach for building capacity. It places leadership in the wider context of building structures, developing processes and changing cultures which act on the system as a whole (O'Leary and Craig, 2007). Improving the progress of individual pupils is dependent on schools developing a culture of high expectations; this is enhanced when it is built into school systems and is part of performance management (Blandford et al., 2011). For leaders this involves a focus on strategic, operational and distributed leadership. Maughan, Teeman and Wilson (2012), in their review of literature related to changing teacher practice, suggest that the strategic vision of good leaders, coupled with high expectations enables teachers to change aspects of their classroom practice. Their findings further showed that effective leaders created a climate supportive of change (operational) and shared responsibility across staff (distributed).

Mourshead, Chijioke and Barber (2010) suggest that systems can get better with 'sustained leadership' and a focus on key practices/processes for systematic improvement. They further highlight a focus on teacher continuing professional development within effective collaborative working models and show the 'cultural shift' in improving educational systems from 'an emphasis on what teachers teach' to 'what students learn' (Mourshead, Chijioke and Barber, 2010: 79). This reflects the approach of the Achievement for All programme, where leadership in schools is enhanced through a collaborative focus on vision, commitment, collaboration and communication.

In creating an environment which supports the learning, development and well-being of all children, the collaborative practice of the staff within the setting needs to be founded on shared values and beliefs, and a shared vision. Most educational settings, whatever their particular constitution, have clear and unambiguous purposes, usually expressed as their vision or mission statement or as values or aims, many of which relate directly to the aims of the school in providing a broad education suitable for children and young people of the twenty-first century. The collaborative development of such statements can provide a firm foundation for cooperative practice within an international educational community.

Achievement for All works with schools to support them in the development of more inclusive approaches. The following case study is an interview with the head teacher of an Achievement for All school. In it he outlines what inclusion means to the school, teachers, parents and pupils.

Case study: Lyng Hall Secondary School, Coventry

Context

Lyng Hall is an Achievement for All Quality Mark Specialist Sports College and Community School. Situated in Coventry, it has 700 students on roll, but has the highest pupil and staff turnover in the city. Attendance is still an issue for the school, especially for pupils identified as SEND. The school is a church school. The proportion of pupils eligible for Free School Meals and those identified as SEND is above average; an above average number of pupils are Statemented. Approximately 30 per cent of pupils at the school are classified as using English as an Additional Language (EAL), with 38 languages represented.

An interview with the head teacher

What does SEND mean to you?

We needed a significant redefinition at Lyng Hall. The SEND register is now only for those with a medical or diagnosable cognitive condition. SEND should not be used to describe issues with behaviour, attendance, underperformance or lack of progress.

What sort of issues has involvement with Achievement for All highlighted and how have you dealt with those?

Achievement for All triggered off a series of questions for us:

- What is the point of the SEND register?
- What is the impact of the IEPs?
- What are the real barriers to learning?
- To what extent should the school take responsibility for the barriers to learning that are attributable to outside school?

What does it mean to you to be an inclusive school?

Being an inclusive school means that all pupils are making better than expected progress. We use data to help children who need staff to change the curriculum for them so they are taught exactly what they need to allow them to achieve their full potential. In my opinion, using current progress trajectories to decide our expectations for pupil progress and exam performance or learning outcomes is dangerous if those expectations are based on the children's rate of progress when they are underachieving.

Take my sixth-form results. Last year, thirty-five children (28 per cent of the total) were accepted by university; yet years ago, when teachers predicted their grades, half of the sixth form had 0 per cent chance of five GCSEs.

Has Achievement for All helped with strategic planning?

Yes, we now use planning to focus on outcomes for specific groups or individuals. The 'one size fits all' policy is no longer used. We are strategically more flexible, and we have to be in order to make sure we provide for each individual child. Our motto is 'Whatever it takes!'

We need a very flexible curriculum if we are going to put the children before the policy or the system. Our system of fifteen associate teachers is key to ensuring that the children come to their lessons, ready and able to learn well. They help the children access the many opportunities available in the school.

Were there any problems?

The main problem was making staff appreciate the value in taking on the problems of the parents. I also worried about my staff's workload but, in a recent Occupational Health Survey, there were no areas of significant stress. The teachers don't mind the hard work I ask them to do, because they can see the effect their actions are having on the lives of the pupils.

How did you communicate Achievement for All within the school?

My senior leadership team has Achievement for All in their job descriptions so it is allied to staff development and performance management. I have a deputy head who ensures the quality of teaching and learning and another who looks after the wider outcomes, such as behaviour and attendance. My heads of department embed Achievement for All in their departmental practice and it is always on the agenda of staff meetings.

With the learning you now have, are there things you would tackle differently?

No. It was huge risk but it has been worth it. The Achievement for All journey has also given me supportive evidence for the recent Ofsted inspection. I also gave the inspectors the Fischer Family Trust data. I keep a detailed portfolio of spiritual, moral, social and cultural evidence, with photos etc., and my self-evaluation form also provided evidence.

Leading change: Monitoring and evaluation

For the most effective outcomes, Achievement for All will need to be an integral part of whole-school self-evaluation and improvement. In the broadest terms, if policy and practice are not monitored it will not be possible to determine whether objectives have been achieved. Monitoring and evaluation is critical to the successful implementation of a policy for Achievement for All. This will involve senior and leadership teams, teachers, teaching assistants, parents, pupils, governors and Local Authorities/ Academy boards (as appropriate). The process of monitoring enables members of the school community to move further towards their agreed objectives. Having adopted a collegial approach to policy development, monitoring and evaluation, the school community can move forward with confidence. A shared vision, strong collaboration, shared communication and whole-school commitment are critical to the success of Achievement for All. Monitoring and evaluation processes must be based on practice and outcomes, and related to agreed criteria/set targets. Furthermore, monitoring and evaluation should provide a framework, whereby leaders, teachers and support professionals can reflect on their own practice and professional needs.

Monitoring Achievement for All

A critical element of the Achievement for All framework is the monitoring and evaluation of individual pupil, class and school progress. If plans are not monitored, it is not possible to determine whether the objectives have been achieved. Monitoring also enables school leaders to obtain the best results from the framework and ensures that the Achievement for All framework is set within the school development/improvement plan. At the heart of the process will be the setting of targets and objectives. Everard, Morris and Wilson (2004: 284) underlines the need for 'yardsticks' by which to recognize when the objectives have been achieved and which can be used 'to set a ratchet to prevent backsliding'.

Monitoring is critical to the successful implementation of plans at any level of practice, strategic or operational. Effective monitoring, which also includes 'managing the processes needed to take corrective action in case of a shortfall' (Everard, Morris and Wilson, 2004: 285), will enable leaders to obtain the best results from the available resources. The process of monitoring will enable leaders and their teams to achieve the agreed Achievement for All objectives.

From clear objectives comes a sense of purpose. It may be difficult to obtain cooperation and agreement when working through objectives; however, it is important to reach agreement within a team if the plan is to work effectively. Once objectives have been agreed, pupils, teachers, parents, leaders and wider support agencies can move forward with confidence. It is important to note that monitoring is an ongoing activity and is integral to teaching and learning: it should not be left to the end of the year. At the same time, 'Plans cannot be revised too often or they lose their value as a secure basis for planning' (Fidler, 2002: 20).

Figure 15.1 illustrates the process of monitoring a plan's progress. It is made easier if objectives are clear and practical and agreed by all members of the team.

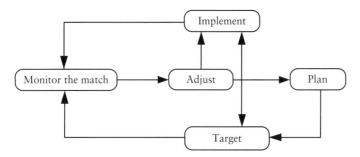

FIGURE 15.1 *Development planning feedback loop*
Source: Hargreaves, 1995

Monitoring Achievement for All provides the basis for evaluating practice, enabling pupils, teachers, parents, leaders and wider support agencies to measure and compare performance against shared criteria and to consider the appropriateness of continuing with the plan. Everard, Morris and Wilson (2004: 285) advocate setting up, 'as part of the overall plan for change', some means of both 'gathering reliable information and analysing it ... in order to measure if the change has been effective and has become truly assimilated'. They highlight the 'future scenario' *description* as a means of ascertaining the appropriate measures to employ. In addition, they suggest that the following techniques can be used as a means of measuring success, where the emphasis is on the 'actual outcomes of the change':

- a checklist of procedures

- a questionnaire about role responsibilities

- an analysis of exam results or an attitude survey to be completed by those most likely to know if the change has been successful, for example, the pupils.

Most significantly, monitoring will provide a framework in which staff can reflect on their own practice, an outcome of which is enhanced learning.

Evaluating practice

Evaluation is a component of development planning and an essential prerequisite to preparing any subsequent plan. Thirty years ago in England the Department for Education and Science (DES, 1989: 17) provided a useful starting point, which is still relevant today; it stated that the purpose of evaluating plans is to

- examine the success of the implementation of the plan.

- assess the extent to which the school's aims have been furthered.

- assess the impact of the plan on pupils' learning and achievement.

- decide on how to discriminate between successful new practices throughout the school.

- make the process of reporting easier.

It is clear that the process of evaluating the impact of a plan on practice is critical to the successful implementation of the plan. It is also useful to heed the advice of Everard, Morris and Wilson (2004: 285) who suggest that an evaluation will highlight any 'unforeseen consequences of the changes' which can subsequently be managed or 'made the subject of further change'.

In contrast to monitoring, evaluation encompasses reviewing the status of a plan's objectives. Through the evaluation process, managers will determine the need to change objectives, priorities and/or practice. As Hall and Oldroyd (1990: 34) explained, evaluation is a collaborative exercise involving

- asking **questions**

- gathering **information**

- forming **conclusions**

- making **recommendations**

Hargreaves and Hopkins (1991) stressed the importance of evaluation in enhancing the professional judgement of teachers on the development of teaching and learning. Evaluation can lead to a change in teachers' perception of their practice; evidence shows how Achievement for All has improved pupil learning by changing the 'behaviours' of teachers.

For leaders the evaluation of plans can provide the basis for action in terms of resourcing, curriculum (development and delivery) and engagement with parents and carers, teachers, pupils and wider professionals.

The final stage in the Achievement for All evaluation process is to report the outcomes. It will be important to consider the purposes of the report as required, against the original goals, context and rationale. At this point leaders will need to consider and report:

- What was the purpose/rationale?

- What is the context?

- What is the content?

- What has been the process? Has this met the needs of parents and carers, pupils, leaders, teachers and wider professionals?

- What are the outcomes against the goals?

- Have there been any unintended outcomes? (positive and negative)

Before disseminating the report, a leader will need to reflect on each process and ensure that only necessary and relevant information is presented.

Summary

By taking a whole-school approach to improvement Achievement for All and the 3As principles leaders have been able to build on, what is in the majority of cases, effective leadership practice and develop this across the school. By changing culture and raising expectations through an effective strategic plan, operationalized through shared ownership, leaders have been able to increase access and raise aspirations and pupil achievement.

This book has described in full how the Achievement for All framework and 3As principles have been introduced and implemented in seven nations. Evaluations have been positive; much has been learnt that is transferable across national and local settings. As educators we have a shared responsibility, a moral purpose to lead evidence-informed change that will impact on the lives of the next generation.

Much can be learnt from testing and learning in different cultural and educational contexts. My own experience, supported by that of others, is that where teachers are committed to all children and young people, learning can take place. The recognition of the most successful teachers that they need to improve in every classroom is what drives them to succeed.

Achievement for All practice is a philosophy sustained by a moral purpose, that continues to be tested, challenged and questioned. It is only by addressing those challenges that the framework will be improved. Two further programmes have emerged from this work; Achieving Early, developed for pre-school and foundation settings, and Achieving Further, developed for post-16 settings. These programmes are subject to the same rigorous review that has shaped the success of the Achievement for All programme.

Achievement for All in International Classrooms has described how to improve outcomes for children and young people identified with SEN and those with disabilities demonstrating that they will achieve because they can irrespective of challenge, need or disadvantage.

REFERENCES

Adomavičius, B., Katiliūtė, E. and Dapkus, G. (2010), *Feasibility Study (Situation Analysis) on the Formal Acquisition of Basic Managerial Competencies and the Informal Upgrading of the Said Competencies*, Lithuania: Centre for School Improvement.

Ainscow, M. (1999), *Understanding the Development of Inclusive Schools*, London: Falmer Press.

Ainscow, M., Booth, T. and Dyson, A. (2004), Understanding and developing inclusive practices in schools: a collaborative action research network, *International Journal of Inclusive Education*, vol. 8, no. 2, pp. 125–39.

Alliance for Excellent Education (2009), Students with disabilities in U.S High Schools, Factsheet, January, Washington: Alliance for Excellent Education.

Angelides, P., Antoniou, E. and Charalambous, C. (2010), Making sense of inclusion for leadership and schooling: a case study from Cyprus, *International Journal of Leadership in Education*, vol. 13, no. 3, pp. 319–34.

Arrowsmith, T. (2007), Distributed Leadership in secondary schools in England: the impact on the role of the headteacher and other issues, *Management in Education*, vol. 2, no. 2, pp. 21–7.

Barber, M. and Mourshead, M. (2007), *How the World's Best Performing School Systems Come Out on Top.* London: McKinsey.

Barber, M., Donnelly, K. and Rizvi, S. (2012), *Oceans of Innovation: The Atlantic, the Pacific, Global Leadership and the Future of Education*, London: IPPR.

Bass, B. M. (1999), Two decades of research and development in transformational leadership, *European Journal of Work and Organisational Psychology*, vol. 8, no. 1, pp. 9–32.

Bateman, B. and Herr, C. M. (2006), *Writing Measurable IEP Goals and Objectives*, Verona, WI: Attainment.

Beany, J. (2006), *Reaching Out, Reaching In*, Nottingham: NCSL.

Blandford, S. (2006), *Middle Leadership in Schools: Harmonising* Leadership *and Learning*, 2nd edn, Harlow: Pearson.

Blandford, S. (2009), *Evaluation of Effective Leadership Programmes*, London: Teach First.

Blandford, S. (2009), *Teach First Master's Programme*, London: Teach First.

Blandford, S. (2011), *The 3As Model: Aspiration, Access and Achievement*, London: Achievement for All.

Blandford, S. (2015), South Korea Blog, available at: https://afaeducation.org/news.php?nid=36

Blandford, S. and Knowles, C. (2013), *Achievement for All: Raising Aspirations, Access and Achievement*, London: Bloomsbury Academic.

Blandford, S. and Shaw, M. (eds) (2001), *Managing International Schools*, London: Routledge.

Blandford, S., Tavlos, L., Williams, K., Crowhurst, M. and Knowles, C. (2011), *Achievement for All Anthology, Pilot 2009-2011*, Nottingham: DfE.

Bloom, S. (ed.) (1956), *Taxonomy of Educational Objectives, the Classification of Educational Goals – Handbook I: Cognitive Domain*, New York: McKay.

Booth, A. and Ainscow, M. (2002), *Index for Inclusion*, Bristol: CSIE.

British Council (2006), National Leadership and school improvement scoping exercise. Report for the British Council, Vilnius, Lithuania.

Busher, H. (2000), The subject leader as a middle manager, in H. Busher and A. Harris with C. Wise (eds), *Subject Leadership and School Improvement*, London: Paul Chapman, pp. 105–9.

Campbell, C., Gold, A. and Lunt, I. (2003), Articulating Leadership values in action: conversations with school leaders, *International Journal of Leadership in Education*, vol. 6, no. 3, pp. 203–21.

Carter, E. (2010), 'What are you Doing After School?' Promoting extracurricular involvement for transition- age youth with disabilities, *Intervention in School and Clinic*, vol. 45, no. 5, pp. 275–83.

Carter, K., Franey, T. and Payne, G. (2006), Reshaping the landscape: exploring the challenges of outward facing leadership with a system perspective, in K. Carter and T. Sharpe (eds), *School Leaders Leading the System: System Leadership in Perspective*, Nottingham: NCSL.

Catsambis, S. (2001), Expanding knowledge of parental involvement in secondary education: connections with high school seniors academic success, *Social Psychology of Education*, vol. 5, pp. 149–77.

Catterall, S. with Dumais, S. and Hampton Thompson, G. (2012), *The Arts and Achievement in At-risk Youth: Findings from Four Longitudinal Studies*, Washington: National Endowment for the Arts.

Children's Society (2015), *The Good Childhood Report 2015*, The Children's Society.

Coe, R., Aloisi, C., Higgins, S. and Elliot Major, L. (2014), *What Makes Great Teaching? Review of the Underpinning Research*, London: Sutton Trust.

Comstock, B. and Ross, S. (2013), An evaluation of the Parent Engagement and Partnership Program Pilot in the U.S: Baseline Implementation Report, unpublished report, Baltimore: The Center for Research and Reform in Education, John Hopkins University.

Constantino, S. (2003), *Engaging All Families*, Lanham, MD: Scarecrow Education.

Cray, D. and Mallory, G. (1998), *Making Sense of Managing Culture*, London: International Thompson Business Press.

CSIE Centre for Studies on Inclusive Education (2011), *Index for Inclusion: Developing Learning and Participation in Schools*, Bristol: CSIE.

Darling-Hammond, L., LaPointe, M., Meyerson, D. and Orr, M. (2007), *Preparing School Leaders for a Changing World: Executive Summary*, Stanford, CA: Stanford University, Stanford Educational Leadership Institute.

De Fraja, G., Oliveira, T. and Zanchi, L. (2010), 'Must Try Harder: Evaluating the Role of Effort in Educational Attainment', *The Review of Economics and Statistics*, vol. 92, no. 3, pp. 577–97.

Department for Education and Science (1989), *Planning for School Development: Advice for Governors, Head Teachers and Teachers*, London: HMSO.

Department for Education and Skills (DfES) (2001), *Inclusive Schooling: Children with Special Educational Needs*, Nottingham: DfES.

Department for Education (2011), *Support and Aspiration: A New Approach to Special Educational Needs and Disability*, Nottingham: DfE.

Department for Education (DfE) (2011), *Training Our Next Generation of Outstanding Teachers: Implementation Plan*, Nottingham: DfE.

Department for Education (2012), *Support and Aspiration: A New Approach to Special Educational Needs and Disability – Progress and Next Steps*, Nottingham: DfE.

Department for Education (2014), *Schools Guide to the 0-25 SEND Code of Practice*, London: DfE.

Department for Education (2015), *Special Educational Needs in England: January 2015*, London: DfE.

Department for Education (2016), *Outcomes for Looked after Children by Local Authorities in England, 31st March 2015*, London: DfE.

Department for Education/Department of Health (2015), *The SEND Code of Practice 0-25*, London: DfE/DoH.

Desforges, C. and Abouchaar, A. (2003), The Impact of Parental Involvement, Parental Support and Family Education on Pupil Achievement and Adjustment: A Literature Review, Department of Education and Skills.

Donnelly, C. (2000), In Pursuit of School Ethos, *British Journal of Educational Studies*, vol. 48, no. 2, pp. 134–54.

Ellis, D. and Hughes, K. (2002), *Partnerships by Design*, Portland, ON: NREL.

Epstein, J. L. (1992), School and family partnerships, in M. Alkin (ed.), *Encyclopedia of Educational Research*, 6th edn, New York: Macmillan, pp. 1139–51.

Epstein, J. L. (1995), School/family/community partnerships caring for the children we share, *Phi Delta Kappan*, vol. 76, pp. 701–12.

European Agency (2016), Lithuania special needs education within the education system, available at: https://www.european-agency.org/country-information/lithuania/national-overview/special-needs-education-within-the-education-system (accessed 01 June 2016).

European Commission (2013), *Support for Children with Special Educational Needs*, Brussels: European Commission.

Everard, K. B., Morris, G. and Wilson, I. (2004), *Effective School Management*, 4th edn, London: Paul Chapman Publishing.

Fidler, B. (2002), *Strategic Management for School Development*, London: Paul Chapman Publishing.

Fink, D. and Hargreaves, A. (2006), *Sustainable Leadership*, San Francisco: Jossey-Bass.

Flouri, E. (2006), Parental interest in children's education, children's self-esteem and locus of control, and later educational attainment: Twenty-Six Year Follow-Up of the 1970 British Birth Cohort, *British Journal of Educational Psychology*, vol. 76, no. 1, pp. 41–55.

Flouri, E. and Buchanan, A. (2004), Early father's and mother's involvement and child's later educational outcomes, *British Journal of Educational Psychology*, vol. 74, no. 2, pp. 141–53.

Fredericks, J. (2012), 'Extra-curricular participation and academic outcomes: testing the over-scheduling hypothesis', *Journal of Youth and Adolescence*, vol. 41, no.3, pp. 295–308.

Fullan, M. (2004), *System Thinkers in Action: Moving beyond the Standards Plateau*, London/Nottingham: DfES Innovation Unit/NCSL.

Fullan, M. (2005), *Leadership and Sustainability: System Thinkers in Action*, Thousand Oaks, CA: Corwin Press and Ontario Principals Council.

Fullan, M. (2007a), *Leading in a Culture of Change*, San Francisco, CA: Jossey-Bass.

Fullan, M. (2007b), *The New Meaning of Educational Change*, San Francisco, CA: Jossey-Bass.

Gibson, S. and Blandford, S. (2005), *Managing Special Educational Needs: A Practical Guide for Primary and Secondary Schools*, London: Sage.

Gold, A., Evans, J., Earley, P. Halpin, D. and Collarbone, P. (2003), Principled principals? Values-driven leadership: evidence from ten case studies of 'outstanding' school leaders, *Educational Management and Administration*, vol. 31, no. 2, pp. 127–38.

Gonzalez, N. and Moll, L. (2002), Cruzando el Puente: *Building bridges to Funds of Knowledge, Educational Policy*, vol. 16, no. 4, pp. 623–41.

Goodall, J., Vorhaus, J., Carpentieri, J., Brooks, G., Akerman, R. and Harris, A. (2011), *Review of Best Practice in Parental Engagement*, Nottingham: DfE.

Goodman, A., Joshi, H., Nasim, B. and Tyler, C. (2015), *Social and Emotional Skills in Childhood and their Long Term Effects on Adult Life: A Review for the Early Intervention Foundation*, London: UCL, Institute of Education.

Gorard, S., Huat See, B. and Davies, P. (2012), *The Impact of Attitudes, Aspirations on Educational Attainment and Participation*, York: Joseph Rowntree Foundation.

Grace, G. (1998), Realising the mission: Catholic approaches to school effectiveness, in R. Slee, S. Tomlinson and G. Weiner (eds), *School Effectiveness for Whom? Challenges to the School Effectiveness and School Improvement Movements*, London: Falmer Press, chapter 9.

Gronn, P. (2000), Distributed properties: a new architecture for leadership, *Educational Management and Administration*, vol. 28, pp. 317–18.

Hall, V. and Oldroyd, D. (1990), *Management Self-development for Staff in Secondary Schools, Unit 4: Implementing and Evaluating*, Bristol: NDCEMP.

Hango, D. (2007), Parental investment in childhood and educational qualifications: can greater parental involvement mediate the effects of socioeconomic disadvantage? *Social Science Research*, vol. 36, no. 34, pp. 1371–90.

Hargreaves, D. H. (1995), 'Self-managing schools and development planning – chaos or control?' *School Organisation*, vol. 15, no. 3, pp. 215–17.

Hargreaves, D. H. (2007), *The True Meaning of System. Leadership*, London: Sage.

Hargreaves, D. H. and Hopkins, D. (1991), *The Empowered School: The Management and Practice of Development Planning*, London: Cassell.

Harris, A. and Goodall, J. (2007), *Engaging Parents in Raising Achievement. Do Parents Know They Matter?* Department for Children, Schools and Families.

Harris, A. and Muijs, D. (2005), *Improving Schools Through Teacher Leadership*, Maidenhead, UK: Open University Press.

Hattie, J. A. C. (2003), Teachers make a difference: What is the research evidence? ACER Annual Conference Building Teacher Quality, Australia.

HMSO (1978), *The Warnock Report*, London: HMSO.

Hopkins, D. (2007), *Every School a Great School*, Milton Keynes: Open University Press/McGraw Hill.

Hogan, R., Curphy, G. J. and Hogan, J. (1994), What we know about leadership, *American Psychologist*, vol. 49, no. 6, pp. 493–504.

House of Commons Committee of Public Accounts (2012), *Oversight of Special Education for Young People Aged 16–25*, London: TSO.

Humphrey, N. and Squires, G. (2011), *Achievement for All: National Evaluation Final Report*, Nottingham: DfE.

Jackson, C. R. (2010), *Levels of Influence: Time for Leaders Project*, Milton Keynes: Open University Press/ McGraw Hill.

Jackson, C. R., Blandford, S., Pranckuniene, E. and Vildziuniene, M. (2011), Time for Leaders: Lithuania's Response to Changing Leadership and Learning in their Schools, *Professional Development in Education*, vol. 37, no. 5, pp. 701–19.

Kanter, R. M. and Corn, R. (1994), Do cultural differences make a business difference? Contextual factors affecting cross-cultural relationships, *Journal of Management Development*, vol. 13, no. 2, pp. 5–23.

Kloosterman, R., Notten, N., Tolsma, J., and Kraaykamp, G. (2011), The effects of parental reading socialisation and early school involvement on children's academic performance: a panel study of primary school pupils in the Netherlands, *European Sociological Review*, vol. 27, no. 3, June, pp. 291–306.

Knapp, M. S., Copland, M. A., Plecki, M. L. and Portin, B. S. (2006), Leading, Learning, and Leadership Support, A Research Report in collaboration with The Wallace Foundation.

Knifsend, C. and Graham, S. (2012), Too much of a good thing? How breadth of extra-curricular participation relates to school-related affect and academic outcomes during adolescence, *Journal of Youth and Adolescence*, vol. 41, no. 3, pp. 379–89.

Kugelmass, J. W. (2003), *Inclusive Leadership: Leadership for inclusion*, New York: New York State University.

Kugelmass, J. W. and Ainscow, M. (2004), Leadership for inclusion: a comparison of international practices, *Journal of Research in Special Educational Needs*, vol. 4, no. 3, pp. 133–41.

Lamb, B. (2009), Lamb Inquiry: special educational needs and parental confidence, DCSF.

Leithwood, K. and Levin, B. (2005), Assessing School Leaders and Leadership Programme Effects on Pupil Learning: Conceptual and Methodological Challenges, DfES Research Report No 662.

Lopez, M. H. (2009), Latinos and Education: Explaining the Attainment Gap, conference presentation.

Mapp, K. L. (2003), Having their say: Parents describe why and how they are engaged in their children's Learning, *The School-Community Journal*, vol. 13, no. 1, pp. 35–64.

Maughan, S., Teeman, D. and Wilson, R. (2012), *What Leads to Positive Change in Teaching Practice?*, Slough: NfER.

Mayrowetz, D. (2008), Making sense of distributed leadership: exploring the multiple usages of the concept in the field, *Educational Administration Quarterly*, vol. 44, no. 3, pp. 424–35.

Menzies, L. (2013), *Educational Aspirations: How English Schools can Work with Parents to Keep Them on Track*, York: JRF.

Metsapelto, R. and Pulkkinen, L. (2012), Socio-emotional behaviour and school achievement in relation to extra-curricular activity participation in middle childhood, *Scandinavian Journal of Educational Research*, vol. 56, no. 2, pp. 167–82.

Ministry of Culture and Education (1992), *General Concept of Education in Lithuania*, Lithuania: Leidybos Centras.

Ministry of Education and Research (2010–11), *Learning Together, Meld. St. 2010–2011, Report to the Starting, White Paper*, Oslo: Ministry of Education and Research.

Ministry of Education and Research (2014), The Education System, available at: https://www.regjeringen.no/en/topics/education/school/the-norwegian-education-system/id445118/ (accessed 08 June 2016).

Mourshead, M., Chijioke, C. and Barber, M. (2010), *How the World's Most Improved School Systems Keep Getting Better*, London: McKinsey.

National Assembly for Wales (2015), Research Paper, Special Educational Needs (SEN)/Additional Learning Needs (ALN) in Wales, June 2015, Cardiff: National Assembly for Wales.

National College for School Leadership (2009), *Achievement for All: Characteristics of Effective Inclusive leadership – A Discussion Document*, Nottingham: NCSL.

NCSL (National College for School Leadership) (2009a), *A Model of School Leadership in Challenging Urban Environments*, Nottingham: NCSL.

NCSL (National College for School Leadership) (2009b), *Achievement for All: Characteristics of Effective Inclusive Leadership – A Discussion Document*, Nottingham: NCSL.

NCSL (National College for School Leadership) (2011), *Achievement for All: Leadership Matters*, Nottingham: NCSL.

National College for Teaching and Leadership (2016), *Closing the Gap Test and Learn: Executive Summary*, London: NCTL.

Northouse, P. (2004), *Leadership: Theory and Practice*, Thousand Oaks, CA: Sage Publications.

Norwegian Ministry of Education and Research (2006), *The Knowledge Promotion*, Oslo: Norwegian Ministry of Education and Research.

Nye, C., Turner, H. and Schwartz, J. (2006), Approaches to Parental Involvement for Improving the Academic Performance of Elementary School Children in Grades K-6. Education Coordinating Group, The Campbell Collaboration.

O'Brien, M. and Shemilt, I. (2003), *Working Fathers: Earning and Caring*, Manchester: Equal Opportunities Commission.

OECD (1998), Review of National Policies for Education, Lithuania: Examinations' Report.

OECD (2010), *PISA 2009 Results: What Makes a School Successful? – Resources, Policies and Practices (Volume IV)*.

OECD (2011a), *Improving Lower Secondary Schools in Norway, Executive Summary*, Paris: OECD.

OECD (2011b), What can parents do to help their children succeed in school? *PISA in Focus 10*.

OECD (2012a), Are students more engaged when schools offer extracurricular activities? *PISA in Focus*.

OECD (2012b), *Let's Read Them a Story! The Parent Factor in Education*, PISA, Paris: OECD.

OECD (2013), *Education Policy Outlook Norway*, Paris: OECD.

OECD (2015), *Education Policy Outlook 2015: Making Reforms Happen*, OECD Publishing. http://dx.doi.org/10.1787/9789264225442-en

OECD (2016a), *Education in Latvia*, Paris: OECD.

OECD (2016b), *Low Performing Students- Why They Fall Behind and How to Help them Succeed*, Paris: OECD.

O' Gorman, E. and Drudy, S. (2010), Addressing the professional development needs of teachers working in the area of special education/inclusion in mainstream schools in Ireland, *Journal of Research in Special Educational Needs*, vol. 10, no. 1, pp. 157–67.

Ofsted (2008a), *Learning Outside the Classroom*, London: OfSTED.

Ofsted (2008b), *Rising to the Challenge: A Review of the Teach First Initial Teacher Training Programme*, London: HMI.

Ofsted (2013), *Unseen Children: Access and Achievement 20 Years On*, London: Ofsted.

O' Leary, D. and Craig, J. (2007), *System Leadership: Lessons from the Literature*, Nottingham: NCSL.

Ortiz, A., Robertson, P. and Wilkinson, C. (2009), Leadership for BESt ERA Model Implementation, Research presented at the BESt ERA Conference, Austin, TX.

Pashiardis, P. and Brauckmann, S. (2009), www.cedol.org/wp-content/uploads/2012/02/120-124-2009.pdf

Peters, T. and Waterman, R. (2004), *In Search of Excellence: Lessons from America's Best-run companies*, London: Profile Books.

Pranckuniene, E. (2009), *Time for Leaders*, Lithuania: Project Conference Presentation.

Pujol, S. J. (2010), Preparing teachers for inclusive education: some reflections from the Netherlands, *Journal of Research in Special Educational Needs*, vol. 10, no. 1, pp. 197–201.

PwC (2013), Social Impact Assessment (Achievement for All): PwC.

PwC (2014), Social Impact Assessment (Achievement for All): PwC.

PwC (2015), Social Impact Assessment (Achievement for All): PwC.

Ruijs, N. M., Van der Veen, I. and Peetsma, T. T. D. (2010), Inclusive education without special educational needs, *Educational Research*, vol. 52, no. 4, December, pp. 351–90.

Schargel, F. P. and Sink, J. (2001), *Strategies to Help Solve Our School Dropout Problem*, Larchmont, NY: Eye on Education.

Schleicher, A. (2014), *What We Learn from the PISA 2012 Results*, Education Today: OECD.

Senge, P. (2007), Collaborating for systemic change, *MIT Sloan Management Review*, Nr. 2, pp. 44–54.

Shaw, B., Bernardes, E., Tretheway, A. and Menzies, L. (2016), *Special Educational Needs and their Links to Poverty*, Joseph Rowntree Foundation.

Silins, H. (1994), The relationship between transformational and transactional leadership and school improvement outcomes, *School Effectiveness and School Improvement*, vol. 5, no. 3, pp. 272–98.

Simonaitienė, B., Leonavičienė, R. and Žvirdauskas, D. (2004), Manifestation of Leader's Communicative and Educational Abilities as a Premise for Learning

Organisation Development in NEWSLETTER Social Science in Eastern Europe, June 2005.

Slee, R., Tomlinson, S. and Weiner, G. (1998), *School Effectiveness for Whom? Challenges to the School Effectiveness and School Improvement Movements*, London: Falmer Press.

Snipiene, R. and Alisauskas, R. (2010), *Comenius Report on Lithuania: A European Qualification Network for Effective School Leadership*, Lithuania: Ministry of Education and Science.

Spillane, J. (2006), *Distributed Leadership*, San Francisco: Jossey-Bass.

Steer, A. (2009), *Learning Behaviour: Lessons Learned. A Review of Behaviour Standards and Practices in Our Schools*, Nottingham: DCSF.

Sutton Trust (2011), *Improving the Impact of Teachers on Pupil Achievement in the UK – Interim Findings*, London: Sutton Trust.

Teach First (2010), Available at: http://www.teachfirst.org.uk

The Annie E. Casey Foundation (2010), 'Why Equal Opportunity is Important'.

TSO (The Stationary Office) (2013), *Children and Families Bill*, London: TSO.

Topor, D., Keane, S., Shelton, T. and Calkins, S. (2010), Parent involvement and student academic performance: a multiple mediational analysis, *Journal of Prevention & Intervention in the Community*, vol. 38, no. 3, pp. 183–97.

UNESCO (1994), *The Salamanca Statement and Framework for Action on Special Needs Education*, Paris: UNESCO.

UNESCO (2005), *Education for All Global Monitoring Report: The Quality Imperative*, Paris: UNESCO.

Utdanningsdirektratet (2013), Information about the Educational and Psychological Counselling Service, available at: http://www.udir.no/Stottemeny/English/Information-about-the-Educational-and-Psychological-Counselling-Service/

Wales Centre for Equity in Education (2015), *Achievement for All Pathfinder schools in Wales, Final Report*, Cardiff: Wales Centre for Equity in Education.

Welsh Assembly Government (2004a), *Children and Young People: Rights to Action*, Cardiff: WAG.

Welsh Assembly Government (2004b), *SEN Code of Practice for Wales*, Cardiff: WAG.

Welsh Government (2012), *Forward in Partnership for Children and Young People with Additional Needs*, Cardiff: WG.

Welsh Government (2014a), *Legislative proposals for Additional Learning Needs*, Cardiff: Welsh Government.

Welsh Government (2014b), *Qualified for Life: An Education Improvement Plan for 3 to 19 Year Olds in Wales*, Cardiff: Welsh Government.

Wenger, E. (1998), *Communities of Practice: Learning, Meaning and Identity*, Cambridge: Cambridge University Press.

Williams, D. L. and Chavkin, N. F. (1989), Essential elements of strong parent involvement programs, *Educational Leadership*, vol. 47, pp. 18–20.

Zwozdiak-Myers, P., Cameron, K., Mustard, C., Leask, M. and Green, A. (2009), Literature review: analysis of current research, theory and practice in partnership working to identify constituent components of effective ITT partnerships, Brunel University, London: TDA.

INDEX